Thank you

Hada

From

Sonia

1

Autobiography

SLAUGHTER BABY

Sonia gisa

I warmly thank Amie Hampsheir-Gill who made the English translation of this book.

The names of several people cited in this work have been changed either for their safety or upon request.

Certain events related in this book which took place during my childhood were not told to me until a few years later by their contributors.

In order to maintain the authenticity and use of the Kinyarwanda language, various proper words are written in their original language, the meaning of which is attached.

PROLOGUE

My gaze scrutinizes the grey of the sky, on this rainy day in June. Nothing can disturb the big drops of water that fall near my window.

In this tiny student room, which I remain in post studies, the chatter of my neighbours disturbs the smooth running of my thoughts. I look left, right, staring at the walls, the furniture, lost in my imagination. I think for the thousandth time to put pen to paper and illustrate the story of my life.

There is no question of romance nor comedy within this autobiography. Only a reflection on its existence, purpose, happiness and my mission on Earth, if there is one.

I sincerely hope that this desire to share my personal ideas and experiences will be a source of inspiration for those who take the time to read my story. So for those who read this, I find my salvation in all of you.

THE ADVENTURE

Today I woke up at dawn, well before the usual time. It's a very special day for me. When you are passionate about your work, everything seems fluid, simple, and nothing is binding anymore. You just have to be punctual and in good shape, like when you do something important for the first time. It seems that with the excitement comes nerves, as I feel a great chill sweep over me. My hands become more sweaty as the minutes pass by, and slowly I feel butterflies begin to flutter in my stomach.

I made sure that today, being a special day, I called the taxi well in advance of my 6 am appointment, settling in the back hastily as the taxi revs its engine. Although the outside always appears greyish at this time, the city remains calm and serene. Around the road pass shrubs of all sizes, as we cross a bridge surrounded by multicoloured leafy hedges. I have the impression of entering a fairytale setting, each shrub seems magic to me, carrying a secret.

Maybe it's because I'm happy. Today is a special day, right?

The driver turns to start the discussion, we discuss everything and nothing. He has already driven me several times and, out of curiosity, asks me where I am travelling to so early in the morning. Indeed, this is not one of my usual destinations.

We are going intramural, but in a secluded location, containing huge film studios. I told him that I had been chosen to play in the future commercial of a global industrial group, Suez. This information arouses his interest and he tells me that he is the father of a 16-year-old girl who dreams of becoming an actress. I remember that at her age, I would have done everything to get advice from someone more experienced than me. I take a long breath of empathy and urge her to start by casting and register with a modelling or acting agency. With a big smile on his face, he thanks me.

I was hovering over my little cloud, but one detail bothered me: a tiny touch of anxiety knowing that everything has an end.

The vapour invaded my sweaty hands, great shivers again run up and down my legs and arms like lightning bolts, bouncing the adrenaline rush throughout my body. The feeling of having butterflies in your stomach will be for much later. This advertisement will be my first to be broadcast on more than 5 television channels in Europe. This is the fateful moment to prove to anyone, myself and the agency included, that I can be trusted I can do this.

Day after day I repeated the text over and over like a broken stereo but was definitely not convinced of the final result. As if the negative comments that had been addressed to me throughout my childhood continued to echo like a bad dream and erode my confidence. I had not been the desired child, not being a boy, and this permanent finding of not being suitable had become a solid base for my low self-esteem. With time and its share of additional frustrations, I had gained the strength to overcome these fears that were not mine, but those of my loved ones. Pre-pubescent, I had a fine, masculine allure, and shy temperament; attributes subject to criticism. Growing up, I became disobedient, and things had not changed in their direction. However, I remained guided by a positive inner force, an intuition which guided me towards my uniqueness, and which forced me to grow and surpass myself.

But back on topic. A friend who had viewed the images pointed out to me that I had a strong accent. Another annoying detail, when you have to recite a text in French and English. But ultimately why worry? I had passed my casting, so that meant that I suited them. Whatever the circumstances, you can never be 100% ready.

It is enough simply to launch out at the desired time with the means at hand, and give the maximum.

When I finally reached the second floor, the entire makeup team was already present. I don't have to do any fittings because that took place yesterday, so it's perfect. It's always strange how this permanent desire to want to be absolutely perfect, which has accompanied me since my first years of fighting to become a model, reappears. Becoming a professional and recognized model had been a great responsibility and a personal challenge. I had overcome my fears with a few psychological crutches, and the search for perfection was one of them. Despite what I imagined of the fashion industry, it turned out that the teams around me were extremely friendly, that everyone was smiling and welcoming. The fashion community has a reputation for being ruthless, ruled by wholly superficial beings, where you are constantly monitored by a thousand eyes. This preconception has proven to be completely false.

During the makeup session, I meet the young man with whom I have to film. All the makeup artists and hairdressers call him by his first name, Pierre, and remember their common shoots. Pierre is almost in his 40s, and already has a lot of experience and ease on set. He's a relaxed actor, really funny. His presence helps me to relax and thanks to him, I survive this 15 hour day where I constantly wonder if I am doing the right thing. Not to mention the psychological fatigue and the freezing cold because of my outfit formed simply of a light dress and a cardigan.

Thank goodness the Stage Manager is coming and going on set to bring me little heated bags. At the end of filming, I ask the stylist if I can keep my filming outfits or buy them. Deep down, I know they will bring me luck, and each time I wear them or look at them, I have a smile of satisfaction as I bag a 50% discount as finally someone from the film crew who drops me off at my place as I am so fatigued from the long day. Exhausted but proud of myself, I know that my dream has come true. If I am asked how I managed to hold these fifteen hours, I will answer that I have not really seen them pass.

Although we did the same scene over and over again, it never ceased to spark my interest. Until today, I have always had infinite patience when it came to a parade, a photoshoot or a casting because I am passionate beyond what you can imagine. It doesn't matter how many hours I have to work since I am immersed in rapture.

This is how it all started. Two weeks ago, I received a phone call from my agency. At that time, I was an office worker for a mundane job and consequently missed their call. During my return to the Metro, I listened to the message on my answering machine; I was booked a job from a casting i did week before, I listened to the message again and again- I couldn't believe it. It was my first casting since I landed a contract in the largest modelling agency in Belgium a month earlier.
It had been a very long process but worth it, as I shall tell you more later in my story.

This opportunity was the first in a long series. Each time, I asked myself the same question:

How did a little girl born in a small village of Rusenge in Rwanda, get there?

It was so far from anything I could imagine. As a child, my head was filled with dreams that were impossible to fulfil, and so many whims occupied my imagination. I knew that none of my dreams could come true where I lived, but I continued to dream. Growing up, I understood that it was essential to imagine and dream constantly to condition your mind to the best dispositions.

WHO AM I ?

If I had been asked this question five years ago, I would simply have described myself as a mere Economics student at a well reputated University In Brussels ULB. A prestigious option which guaranteed me a bright future once I completed my course. In September 2012, I started my first year with great enthusiasm and determination to succeed.

Although the course was exciting, I struggled in my first year, leading me to repeat the first term with success and regain self- confidence. Alas, the second term did not go as well, and I ended up with more than four exams to repeat after the summer. I was educated to become independent, without any family financial assistance, but pressure began to build as I fell further and further behind.

At this point I couldn't think carefully about my future, my situation was getting more and more difficult, and my interest in my studies was rapidly decreasing. I wanted to travel, to discover the world, maybe even to do humanitarian work. I yearned to have fun and kick back like everyone else I knew, but instead, I was just counting the minutes, even seconds, until my Master's degree was finally over. Having watched those close to me struggling to secure a decent job, even with a great education, I thought to myself.

Surely there are other ways to succeed?

At this moment I remembered a book I read in my first year of University which greatly inspired me; the life of the great chemist Ernest Solvay. He had a childhood illness that had prevented him from pursuing higher education and instead began working for his uncle. During this time, he made a major discovery by experimenting with new chemical processes.

A few years later, he founded his own company, which had quickly become a pillar of the global chemical industry. This man, who was a reference among academics, had not studied at university, what a revealing irony!

By the time I was 23, I had already been a model for four years. Fashion is a complex and sometimes harsh world where 23 years old can be considered as an advanced age. In principle, it corresponds to the peak of the model's career. I was always told:

You have to have something extra, charisma, charm.

But what does that mean? I was convinced that I was unique and different, having always been attracted to everything out of the ordinary. I dared to take risks in my styling, contrasting colours, clothing and eccentric hairstyle choices. I did receive a lot of criticism for my choice, but you never get noticed for just playing it safe.

I entered as many fashion contests as I could, with little other way to investigate the customs and practices of this industry. Most of the time there was a large cost, as I was unable to obtain a sponsor and had very little support from my loved ones. They never came to any of the parades, even when I bought tickets for them. So I worked, and trust me when I say I worked hard.
I worked in restaurants at the belgian seaside, I dived at Le Grand Café on the embankment of Blankenberge for example, and then I invested every last penny in competitions. If I entered the semi-finals, I had to find a sponsor to participate or pay 150€, then 600€ in the event of a final. For the portfolio book, we had to finance the purchase of 6 photos, each of which cost 30€. But in every contest I participated in, I always won at least one prize. With every success I felt incomparable joy, beyond reality; I was living my dream. I treasured every moment of these competitions, meeting celebrities, being featured on television and working with all the fantastic and famous photographers I had seen in magazines.

From the grand decor to the great cheers of the crowd, not to forget the tension of the final stages! It was as if I had found heaven on Earth.

Of course, it wasn't just me feeling this way, every candidate shared my passion for modelling and dreams of a glittering career, each coming from a unique background. I learned a lot from the others, I diversified my taste and my thoughts, and I made many real friends from this experience. My desire to live this magic forever shone stronger than any fears of appearing before an audience. I had to go the extra mile in the hope that one day I may reach the top, and inspire others in the future just as I was to begin this journey. This is what motivated me, and this I where I felt my future lie, continuing this path through contacts leading to many fashion shows and photoshoots for years to come.

In the summer of 2014, I finally decided to stop my studies. I had to pursue my passion, and nothing else. My family condemned this action, saying that I had missed my chance in life, and I had only been met with failure. According to them, the last choice I had left was to study nursing. Being a young woman of African descent, nursing was the only area that could assure me a financially stable future; a profession with a shortage of personnel where you could be hired regardless of your skin colour.

Like a broken record I was told again and again to forget my dreams, they will never pay my bills, and remember where I am from. Yes in Rwanda we had lived a poor, hard life where any dreams such as this would've been immediately slashed, but this was a whole new country with new opportunities? Nevertheless, with my new life choices, I became and remained the rotten apple in the basket for my family, with no stability for what the future held.

I did follow their reasoning for a time, albeit wrongly. The weight of their expectations prevented me from discovering, assuming and exploring myself, but the time for emancipation was not far off. I still don't know who I am completely, but I'm going to tell you who I think and know I am:

"Another girl! "

I was born on January 10, 1991, in Rwanda. I was not welcome, being the fourth girl in a family desperate to have a boy, as you can tell from my paternal grandmother's exclamation.

Fortunately for my family, two years later my little brother Dieudonné was born. I loved him very much, not just for the fact that he was a boy. You have to believe that my grandmother's hard prayers had finished convincing God to give us a son.

I was raised in Rusenge, a small village which used to be called a "cell" at the time. Above the cell was the sector, then larger than the sector, the commune. Ours was called Bwakira and its prefecture Kibuye, surrounded by nature, far from everything- a breath of fresh air!

All the houses in the village were surrounded by a field of bananas, not only to support the soil and prevent flooding but also they contain very nutritious plantains which make all kinds of juices. To do this, a few strong men grab barley and crush it with "Ishinge" herbs, then it is filtered and boiled. You can also place the juice before boiling it in a large jug and add crushed sorghum flour (which serves as yeast), then burying it wrapped in banana leaves for three days.
Thanks to this process, the mixture turns into a traditional Rwandan beer called Urwagwa, served in the village bars.

Selling Urwagwa to village bar owners allows some villagers little luxuries with the extra money, buying clothes and things they cannot grow. Beyond our banana field extended several other fields which we owned.

There were also three other fields in the Kanogo Valley where sweet potatoes were planted. The latter needs a lot of water and does not grow everywhere. Their flavours vary depending on the soil in which they were planted. During the seed season, we hired a few workers and let the grass grow on half the surface so our cows could graze. The barks of sweet potatoes, bananas and many other plantations were also used to feed the cows, animals which made me so happy as a little girl. Every morning I was up and eager at my father's door so that he would go and extract the milk from the cows, and I always drank the delicious first glass.

My big sister and I were 5 years apart, so when I was born she had started her primary studies. Instead, I spent a lot of time with my parents because the village did not have a nursery school. Most of the women in the village who lived off the field crops took their children with them. During this time, there were no big brothers or sisters to watch us, we wandered freely swallowing what was passing under our noses, earthworms and mud included. At least I hope this has helped strengthen our immune systems, or our sense of taste.

As a child, I noticed a kind of strange scar on the side of my little finger, and one day I asked what could have happened. Despite all the nonsense I had done, I did not remember anything that could have cost me such a scar. I was told that I had been born with six fingers. Out all of the things I thought it could be, this was something that I never would have guessed. I took the news of this amputation very badly; the idea of having 12 fingers seemed so much more fun. On one hand, the operation had been so successful that there was no visible scar. I demanded valid arguments which justified this decision. Why only ten? I knew several children with more than ten fingers, and they were doing very well.

It is true that aesthetically, the sixth finger did not have the finest of appearances. With only five phalanges at the level of the fingers, the sixth finger is found slightly hooked on the little finger and hangs, at the mercy of the slightest hazard.

It is strongly advised to remove it to prevent it from becoming infected. I was told about the process which had made it possible to separate me from this troublesome appendage. It was tightly tied with a wire, then after a few days, it fell on its own, as if it had faded. Even after being told this procedure and its awkward appearance, I still believed that I had been denied a chance to be special and different. This changed as I grew up, as I realised how grateful I was to not have to deal with the pain at a later stage in life. None of the children born in hospitals had more than ten fingers.

The problem was resolved before they left the hospital. The only ones who looked after them were the children born at home. Home births happened quite often, we didn't have phones to call an ambulance, let alone a car to get to the hospital. The village had set up a mutual aid system to transport people to the hospital in the event of an extreme emergency, but that was not enough. Even though some home births were going well, there was still a high rate of death at childbirth.

PRAYER

I will never forget this April 1994 when my whole world turned upside down. I was just 3 years old, an innocent child completely unprepared for what was about to sweep across our village.

The genocide had begun...

The death of our President Juvenal Habyarimana echoed through our crackly radio, but the news sounded, the adults immediately understood what was to follow. My father was certain that war would be declared. An environment of fear had taken over our lives like wildfire, and I, just a little girl, could not even begin to imagine what was about to dawn upon us.

That evening, my father and mother gathered my three sisters and I in the living room. We turned on the kerosene lamps and closed all the windows for fear of being heard, but we didn't talk about much, we mostly whispered.

The genocide had begun.

My father was a non-practising Christian and belonged to the Presbyterian church, which was quite popular after Catholicism. My mother came from a very active family of Seventh-day Adventists. She had to convert to marry my father. Once married, she no longer practised as much, but sometimes took us to the Adventist church on Saturdays. We used to pray before meals and even whenever we were going to travel. However, when it hit our country motivations greatly increased to become closer to God. One day when we were sitting in our dark, little living room, I was chosen to pray. Unlike my little brother, I was old enough to be able to say a prayer. I took the floor:

"Oh God, come before us to cut down the trees and make a path for us....".

My prayer was stopped dead by the urgency to flee. Ironically, these words asked for exactly what we needed at the time.

When I look back, it all seems rather strange to me. How could a 3-year-old child be able to recite this kind of prayer? It will remain a mystery and yet images come to my mind. At this age, is it possible to remember such specific events?

My little prayer brought us great luck because in our desperate flight not one of us stumbled on the slightest root during our entire exodus. When we left our house, we gave up everything, except for a big battery-powered radio that my father kept permanently lit on his shoulder to follow the situation. This is the last image I have of him, and it will never leave me. We were under the cypresses trees of our garden, ready to run at any moment, and he was clutching his silver radio against his right shoulder, listening carefully to what was said, his face tense, and his gaze lost. My three big sisters, aged 14, 12 and 9 were able to embark on a journey, but for me, it was going to be more difficult.

The decision was quickly made that my mother would carry Dieudonné on her back and that I would ride on the back of my 14-year-old sister.

My father refused to flee in the same direction as us. This decision was heartbreaking, but he was aware that men and young boys were the first targets. If the Interahamwe (a name given to the killers) found us with him, no one would be spared. While a woman and children had a chance to inspire pity, although many were killed. The men, all of them, had to be exterminated to prevent the race from perpetuating.

We stayed together, my sisters, my mother and I, and my father took a different path saying to us: "Separate and disperse as much as possible, it would be a shame if everyone was killed in one bite. With these words our paths separated, he left first with his radio, and it was the last moments when I saw the face of my father, whose memory remains blurred. He was assassinated two days later.

My father was a loved and esteemed man in our village. His generosity, his natural propensity to help his neighbour without expecting anything in return had earned him the nickname "Gentle Man". The image I have of my father may be idealized, because of his premature death. I remember my father so beautifully, tall and always benevolent, unable to harm a fly. He often disagreed with the punishments our mother inflicted on us, even when it was deserved. His kindness earned him grudges from some people with short sight.

One day while he was walking and the rain started to fall, he saw a woman carrying her baby on her back and walking in the rain. He went to the nearest store to buy an umbrella and offered it to the woman. A few days later, the woman's husband knocked on our door, furious, asking for whom my father was taking gifts to his wife.

At the time of the genocide, my father had hoped in the back of his mind that all those people he had helped would spare him. Alas, he had overestimated their humanity and their courage during this time. According to the testimony of one of the Interahamwe who participated in his capture, his executioners laughed saying that they were going to kill the "Gentle Man".

Long before Rwanda was evangelized, there was a culture of "Kunywana". It was a pact between two people, often men, a sacred contract sealed for life between two true friends. It consisted of cutting oneself to make his friend drink a little of his blood and vice versa as a pledge of understanding. After this pact, betrayal was unthinkable, including for the descendants. Because of the diseases that this process could spread, this culture has now disappeared. I always wonder if at the time of the genocide this custom was still respected. It was rumoured that my father's ancestors had made a Kunywana pact with the ancestors of the alleged killers.

My mother had a lot of trouble separating us and decided that we will all stay together. To life, to death! After all, she felt it was not worth it if one of us survived while the rest were dead. What sad and unhappy existence would he have left then?

Although the massacres started in Kigali on April 7, 1994, our village was only affected 5 days later. Some villagers wanted to stay at home and did not think the massacres would extend to us. History had proved them right before, but the series of massacres in 1959 and 1963 were far from the genocide of 1994. Most Tutsis or Hutus opponents had been able to flee to Uganda, Zaire, and other neighbouring countries. For our part, the decision was already made to leave to hide.

On leaving the village, the corn and sorghum fields were approaching their harvest in most mountains and valleys. Our first destination was a large plateau called Gikombe, located 500 metres from our house. We hid in the nearest bushes, thinking that the attack would not last long and that it might be possible, with discretion, to fetch food from our house later. It was the great rainy season which extends from March to May in the land of a thousand hills, a torrential rain, always brief, which generally gives way quickly to a big blue sky. In addition to the rains, it was cold and I got the flu and kept sneezing. My sneezing became a real problem and exposed us to the risk of being spotted.

Once we were hiding in a sorghum field, my mother heard the noise of the killers and their dogs in the distance and put her hand on my mouth as I was about to sneeze. I struggled to be able to breathe as my nose was blocked but my mother forbade me to speak. Not listening to her, I asked,

"So when am I going to speak?

And she whispered,

"When Jesus returns."

I took his message very seriously and from that moment on I did not sneeze or say a word until Jesus was back.

The situation in our village worsened, the Tutsi who had stayed at home were all killed. The looting of the houses had been total, stocks of food, clothing, money, some had even taken the French windows and the sheets that covered the houses. The troops called "Igitero" grew rapidly in numbers and composed of many men equipped with machetes, knives, Ubuhiri and hatchets, anything strong enough to snatch away life. In my village, they often moved by singing victorious songs which told how God had offered our lives, that the Tutsi were snakes, and that all snakes had to be killed by crushing their heads.

In 1959 and 1963, they only ransacked the homes of the fugitives, and most of the Tutsi returned when calm was restored.

This is the reason why some of our neighbours had not fled, they did not imagine that the new objective was extermination. This time, even some Hutu married to Tutsi did not hesitate to murder their spouses. There was no longer any mercy, several Hutu women who were pregnant with Tutsi were disembowelled by the Interahamwe.

As all the bushes had been cut, there was nowhere to hide near the village. One day when we were all hiding in a banana field, a close noise was heard. It was the end, the killers had flushed us out. One of my sisters rushed behind a banana tree further. We were frozen in fear, my mother could not run with my little brother on my back and me in her arms. We expected them to land in front of us and kill us. A few minutes later, all was eerily still. False alarm, my sister, who had been watching behind her hiding place for a while, came back to us. At that time my mother repeated to us the importance of staying together no matter what. That it was useless for one of us to survive and not the others, to die together or to survive together, nothing else.

Friday, April 15, we left in the direction of the neighbouring town where the massacres had not yet spread. We crossed the Nyabarongo River, which served as a mass grave. The killers hoped that the corpses would float to Ethiopia, which they considered to be the real country of the Tutsi.

We went to our paternal aunt in Masango, a neighbouring commune belonging to the prefecture of Gitarama. Our aunt had married a Hutu, they hid us for two nights. The first day, we ate Pondu a popular east african meal and the second day everyone fell ill: diarrhoea, vomiting, ... My mother went behind the house to pray and passed a neighbour to whom she told that her children were very bad. Despite the antipathy between the two neighbouring families, this woman, who also had children, offered her milk which was drunk the same evening while eating. The next day, we had regained strength.

The troops approached the village of Masango, so we left in a hurry the morning of Monday, April 18. The same day, we took refuge in the Karambi commune office where we slept and then had to leave quickly the next day because of the proximity of the troops. They still had heart, in Karambi, there were other refugees.

After walking for a few hours, sometimes hiding, we arrived at the headquarters of a congregation of religious brothers in Byimana. There were already several refugees there, we slept two nights on the premises of a school, and the Interahamwe were still getting closer. The Brother Director wishing to protect each of us swore on behalf of the Lord to accompany all the refugees to Kabgayi, another seat of the religious brothers made up of a secondary school. He got into his car at the start of the procession and drove ahead of us. On April 21, 1994, the crowd followed him to the Saint Joseph Kabgayi school group.

This school located shortly before the town of Gitarama is close to a road which links Butare and Kigali, the capital of Rwanda. There was Kabgayi Hospital, one of the best known in the country, and a small dirt road that gave access to the Saint-Joseph school group, managed by the Joseph Brothers. Its buildings formed a square which encompassed a small chapel, two volleyball courts, a basketball court, gardens, and an empty field which would be used years later for outdoor parties.

Inside the school, the group dispersed into several classes. The windows in our classroom offered a view of the highway, and we were all huddled and lying day and night on the cement floor. Access to the kitchen was organized in turn for each man and woman according to a defined schedule. Some women, when it was their turn, took their children into the kitchen to feed them at will. My mother didn't find it fair.

The Joseph Brothers were doing everything possible to prevent the killers from entering to massacre us. Their argument for limiting access to school was that they feared buildings and classrooms were filled with corpses and traces of blood, that it could damage the school, and be expensive to repair. They agreed that the killers could come and take a few people at any time, provided that they kill them outside the establishment. On the days when killers wanted to go to school, we didn't eat as fear kept us from moving.

At first, they were only interested in men and young boys. I remember a former colleague of my mother, in the same class as us, whom we had helped to hide. We often covered him with a blanket on which we would sit together. Sometime after the genocide, I met him at the hospital where he worked, he suffered from back problems, consequences that were certainly caused by all the times that we sat on him to save him. He was eternally grateful to us and saw his pain as a blessing.

As the days passed, the food provided by the school was practically exhausted and the water was cut off. I was terribly hungry, we would die slowly. One evening I went out to an electrically lit outdoor garden, and in the middle of the night, I began to eat the herbs in the garden. Some had a good salty taste, and I was satisfied with it. My mother woke up that night and noticed that one of her children was missing. After searching for me everywhere, she finally saw me through the large, curtainless windows in the classroom.

The other refugees in our class called me "I'm hungry" because I kept repeating this phrase over and over again day and night. When my cries and cries became unbearable, my mother gathered all my sisters and me to go and pray outside in a corner. After that prayer, I felt soothed and stopped crying and back in the classroom, I was transformed. The others asked, "What then gave your child? And my mother replied with silence.

I still wonder how we were able to survive without food and water. At the very beginning, the killers had not yet landed in mass. Men and women from time to time cooked, we ate the cornmeal dough preparation that the school has in its stocks. Then there were fewer and fewer men and the dough was coming undercooked because of the killers who often interrupted the cooks. Our only food was no longer available, stocks exhausted. With the survival instinct always strongest, I quickly understood that certain salted herbs from the garden were edible and nutritious and I picked them from time to time. The garden where they grew was not very clean, all the parents went there to deposit their children's excrement. This natural fertilizer was certainly the secret of their generous growth ... This makeshift salad allowed me to survive for many days.

The inhabitants of Gitarama were the most generous in the country. Some of the refugees came from the area and their former neighbours hid to bring them food or other small things.

We were sometimes lucky enough to receive one or two sweet potatoes for the meal in return for my mother's small sewing jobs.

They were the first to hide, at the risk of their lives, the maximum of their Tutsi friends and neighbours. It's thanks to the food that my mother managed to give us a little something now and then. While examining my conscience, I wonder about the incredible strength and courage shown by some Hutu opponents despite the general propaganda. All the other fugitives in the country who hoped to find refuge in houses of God or religious schools did not all have our luck. Our protectors, the Joseph Tutsi brothers, were also killed, like Louis, whose task was to stay at the gate to give the little exit papers to refugees.

Two endless months of sorrow and sadness, staying day and night numb from exhaustion, on a cement-covered floor where if a rat or other had bitten us, we wouldn't even have reacted.

AFTER THE STORM

The RPF Inkotanyi militias rescued us on June 2, and we left Kabgayi. A few days before, the son of a refugee woman named Emerancienne (my mother's friend during their secondary studies in Remera-Rukoma) had been killed. Other young boys were put on buses to be killed in Gisenyi, a province in the south of the country where the war was still going on. The RPF Inkotanyi militiamen were few in number and progressed from region to region, without being able to take the whole country at once. We were forced to progress towards regions pacified by the national front while they continued towards the regions still occupied.

We landed at Mugina W'imvuzo, still in the Gitarama region. Towards the south, in the province of Butare, dysentery had spread due to lack of hygiene.

My little brother Dieudonné was completely dehydrated, and his mouth was constantly wide open. However, he had survived all this difficult time in class, and now his tongue showed bloody breaks.

Two days later, on the way to Ruhango, my mother, who had nothing to breastfeed Dieudonné, put her saliva in his mouth to try to hydrate him. He cried, then after a short silence, he succumbed.

I remember the adorable and lovable baby he was, today he would certainly be a young man of college age, or of getting married. When I think about it, I remember the strong resentment that had stirred me the day of his birth. I realized with bitterness that I was no longer going to be the youngest, the darling of my parents. Today I strongly feel guilty for having carried such thoughts.

My bruised heart, my mother wrapped him in a scarf and cherished him for the last time, without saying a word. We were certain that we were crossing the Calvary of Jesus, carrying the cross on which he was going to be crucified. She walked away in silence, and at the approach of a bush, placed him just behind. It was impossible to bury him in dignity, we barely had the strength to walk. She stayed with him for a moment, the time to say a little prayer, then like zombies, we resumed our journey.

We stayed in Ruhango for a week, then reached Kinazi, where we were able to find something to eat.

My mother made friends with a refugee from Gitarama. One day, they followed men to help them harvest bananas, with the aim of also profiting from them. They cut the bananas still green, dug to keep them warm underground, wrapped in banana peels. Four days later, the bananas were ripe. The men made banana juice while my mother and her friend took care of crushing sorghum to make yeast. The mixture made it possible to draw several cans of beer which they transported together to the small village where we were staying. It was agreed with the men that my mother and her friend could keep the cans they had transported. Once in the village, the men gave them only one can each, and they hurried to sell it at the risk that the men would eventually take them back. With the beer money, we bought some body moisturizer and a soap. After long months without taking a single shower, we were finally able to wash. After a week in Kinazi, we joined Bugesera. The month of July was approaching, we occupied a deserted house. My mother had found a little job where she sewed closures from large bags of goods. In the fields abandoned by their owners, we ate food and in the streets, a few objects lying around. Much of the summer passed, and when the country was finally liberated, a place was placed in one of the large trucks for Kibuye.

We had to walk the rest of the way back to Rusenge, and in the huge, disorganized and abrupt crowd of refugees, I lost my mother and two sisters. I found myself alone with my oldest sister.

Our family was very large, my paternal grandfather had married more than three women who had given him many children. After the war, the survivors were counted on the fingers of one hand. A few weeks later, we found one of our aunts and two daughters, who looked after us from that day on.

I returned home on September 5, 1994. We were not surprised to find our house completely destroyed. She was missing the roof sheets, windows, doors, cows and everything in the house. There remained only a half-standing carcass, spotted with brown spots because of the bricks that the rain had caused to sink. Repairing the other half to be able to live there as quickly as possible was necessary.

The workers added the missing bricks to the carcass, laid a makeshift roof and replaced the windows and doors. During this time we had found a temporary home which belonged to people who had fled the RPF to avoid prison. It was a house with walls riddled with holes, you could see us distinctly from the outside.

This house was filthy, to the point that we all contracted scabies, a very painful disease, accompanied by fevers, and itching. The hardest part was the endless nights when I no longer knew where to sleep. My aunt applied a purple liquid all over my body that made me cry from pain, and the showers were tortured. The treatment worked after a few weeks, and I was able to find a brand new body.

When our house was finally finished, one of my two cousins sacrificed a year to take care of the house and the kitchen since my aunt had found a job at the Kilinda hospital. My father was no longer there, as was my little brother. The course of our existence had been turned upside down and degraded. A friend and colleague of my aunt whose big brother was sub-prefect of the prefecture of Kibuye brought us clothes: sweaters and little dresses especially for me. There were even small shoes, I was the only one in the family to have shoes. Every Saturday we went to church, hope was back.

There was a morbid story circulating about one of our former neighbors to Rusenge, a man named Masenge. You could still see his feet sticking out of a ditch that used to be a toilet.

He had been thrown there head first. The killers had kept him alive until the last moment so that he could remember what a Tutsi looked like, then eliminated him at the last minute when they learned that the Inkotanyi were on their way to liberate the Village.

RETURN TO NORMAL

Due to lack of money, our house in Rusenge was far from complete. The new walls had been erected on the ruins of the old ones and some room doors were still missing. The rest of the amenities were the bare minimum.

Our grandmother also returned from exile. I don't know how she managed to hide and survive. She lived with her daughter, my maternal aunt, her only surviving child. The latter was one of the Rwandans who had taken refuge in Congo, crossing the country on foot.

Very shortly before the war broke out, my aunt became engaged to a young man. They were a wonderful couple and had gone together to take refuge in Congo. The country was overcrowded, most lived in hastily set up camps. When they left, they lost sight of themselves among the huge and brutal crowd and never met again. No one knows if her fiancé has survived. It took my aunt a long time to turn the page.

Returning from exile several years later, she remained single for a long time, and could not forget it.

Many exiles took months and sometimes years to realize that the war was really over. During this time, an immense sorrow had invaded the heart of my grandmother. All of her family members in Gikongoro had been killed, and she also believed that all of her other children were dead. My father's murder had been certified, people had been charged and sentenced for his murder and were already in prison. Her younger son had also been killed, and after a year passed, she had no hope of seeing her daughter again. Yet there was nothing to show the sadness on her face.

I believe that in the extreme moments of life, we realize that we are still there, and we accept that life continues.

My paternal grandmother was the only one of my grandparents who was still alive. No one was left on my mother's side. My two grandparents, my three uncles and an aunt were all dead, and it is unknown when and how it all happened.

Grandmother was my grandfather's youngest wife and also the last in a long list. He owned a lot of land, and each woman had her side of the mountain, which was quite rare. My grandmother was a very pretty woman with light skin and long black curly hair. Aware of her beauty, she enjoyed taking care of herself.

With a fairly disinterested soul and harsh temperament, she had lost a few babies before the birth of my father, whose birth was truly a miracle. Later, she had my aunt and my youngest uncle Niyonshuti who died during the genocide.

Before the war, there were some tensions between my mother and my grandmother who had managed to scare away many of my father's girlfriends. For her, her son was so handsome that no woman on earth could match him. She therefore had an automatic and arbitrary antipathy towards my mother who, having been brought up in the wisdom of religious values, had paid little attention to it.

The old quarrels did not prevent us from spending our days with grandmother, who still loved her grandchildren. We did not stay long in Rusenge, it was too far from the Kilinda hospital where my aunt worked. We moved near the hospital, to a small town close to all the necessary amenities, to a house on the side of the road. It was small and dirty, without cement on the ground, and colonized by fleas. There was a small kitchen outside but without a fence, and all the passers-by could see us with our pots and pans. It was a small town under reconstruction where there were other refugees living there, we felt safe there.

Kilinda hospital had several buildings to house workers at low cost. We were placed on the best side of the hospital, a neighborhood near a nursing school and a kindergarten where important people lived. Next to us was a large house where a widow of the genocide and her three daughters lived. In another large house lived another widow and her four young sons. The youngest of his boys was born at the beginning of the massacres, and had lived his first months of life in shelters. When I met him, he was a very sensitive little boy who got angry often and who cried for nothing, he was afraid of everything, he was born in fear.

None of these widows had remarried and we often played at home with their children. Our house was the smallest of all, much less than half of the other two, but it was warm. It consisted of a large and only room in the middle of which we had placed curtains to make a bedroom and a living room. I had decorated this curtain by hanging a multitude of drawings on it that I had cut out during my kindergarten lessons.

On the other side of the curtains there were two beds, one where my aunt and I slept, and another where my aunt's daughters slept. My sister lived next door at the nursing school boarding school.

I started nursery school in 1996 at the age of 5. Because of this late start, I was placed directly in the last year. A few months later, the teacher realized that I had never said a word. She told my aunt who was surprised, she had never paid attention. Then thinking about it, she realized that I had stopped talking for a while. She asked me why and I replied confidently: "Jesus has not yet returned, Mom had told me in the bushes when they were hiding that I will not speak until Jesus returns. "

Moved, she reassured me: "You can start talking again now." I started talking again little by little, sometimes with an ounce of fear that I couldn't control. Even today, I sometimes experience this strange blockage when faced with stressful situations.

At that time, NGOs came in droves to Rwanda. One of them, specialized in the field of Health, had come to reinforce the hospital of Kilinda. Several hospital cars were named after the NGO, as were the boxes containing the medicines. They also distributed large boxes containing protein cookies for children suffering from malnutrition. I particularly remember a young Belgian doctor named Hilde Proot, employed by one of these NGOs. She had become a great friend of my aunt and often came to visit us.

We loved taking pictures together and sometimes she started to cry when she saw the conditions in which we lived, in this very small house. Hilde had offered to pay for my sister studies at the nursing school, and my aunt had accepted.

Her house was close to ours, she often organized events, receptions where she invited all the families in the neighborhood. Hilde came to pick me up regularly to spend some time with her. Although we did not speak the same language, she took the time to tell me reassuring things in order to cure me of my trauma. She had given me a wonderful children's book called "Madame de bonne famille": The story of a woman who had many cats as her family. Her two older children were called Duchesse and Marie, and they had kittens. Duchesse was my favorite, so that about 6 years later, I adopted a black cat with green eyes and gave it the first name of Duchesse.

Hermans, a lady from Germany, was raising funds from her "Rhineland-Paratinate" region to finance the purchase of back-to-school supplies for the surviving children. In kindergarten, I quickly caught up with my classmates.

Then in elementary school in Kilinda, I was lucky to be with my cousins and the children of our neighbors with whom we had become very close, all our parents worked at the hospital in Kilinda.

After the genocide, many orphanages opened their doors. Sometimes children and their families simply got lost when they left the camps, swept away by the frenzy of the crowd. So regularly, a magazine specially dedicated to the lost published photos of children or people who were looking for their families. In addition to a photo, there were their names and ages at the time of the incident. This allowed some parents to find their children and vice versa. All those who had not seen the bodies of their loved ones directly, still hoped to find them one day in this review. There were also some pictures of children that we saw years after years.

One day, the hospital had the idea of selling all the laying hens on one of their farms at bargain prices to their employees. Our neighbor bought two hens for her two youngest daughters and my aunt bought one for me. They were our first post-war animals. We were so happy that we had all given them names according to their appearances: one of those which belonged to the neighbor had lost her feathers at the level of the neck, which had earned her the name "Neck".

The other was an awkward hen that banged everywhere and missed all the insects within reach. She was fat and full of excrement. She was nicknamed "Painetta" after the clumsy hero of a school book. My hen was called "Young" because she was fast, dangerously perennial and always ventured far too far. So much so that the owner of a garden that she had messed up struck her a fatal blow. We found her dead behind our outdoor kitchen a few days later. We weren't used to eating animals that died that way.

ADVENTURER OR SIMPLE VICTIM ?

As soon as I was old enough to walk, I never missed a chance to hurt myself. It was involuntary of course, I just wanted to experience the craziest and impossible things. As awkwardness and stupidity are my only attributes at this point, many people have to wonder if I will grow up well one day. This behavior cost me many scars, and not the least. I was calm in my words, while my actions bordered on a permanent accident. Among all the other kids in the neighborhood, I was one of the youngest, so while the older ones were playing ball or jump rope, we were playing dolls, mimicking the sequence of complex cooking recipes in small jars of tomato sauce.

It sounded harmless, but it was a real role-playing game,

which became much more interesting when the grown-ups interfered in our staging.

One day we played hospital games, which consisted of swallowing raw beans with a glass of water. Exactly as if they were drugs prescribed by the doctor. When the grown-ups returned from their school day and learned about our game, they told us that raw beans were dangerous, that it was absolutely essential to neutralize their deadly effects by drinking at least two liters of water. Two liters of water, for children from 5 to 7 years old, it was almost impossible, it represented what we could drink in several days. We did our best, but none of us managed to drink more than a liter.

We all ended up like barrels, rolling almost on the ground in spite of ourselves, our limbs swollen and motionless like balloons. Lying down, saturated with water in our flooded stomachs, we were waiting for a certain death which would come either from drowning, or from raw beans which had not received their full two liters.

When our parents came home from work, they weren't too worried, and they even lent themselves to the game, exclaiming: "It was not the brightest idea to drink so much water! What do you think? When you swallow raw beans and drink lots of water afterwards, well you just water them, and they will grow even faster in your belly! "I panicked, my imagination got carried away. In my small manipulable mind appeared very convincing images of a bean growing in my stomach, its roots coming out through my mouth like wriggling lianas, it was terrifying. It is true that I had not yet studied human anatomy, and that I knew nothing about the digestive system. So I drank their words, which further watered all these evil raw beans. Days and months passed, and the beans had still not grown, we felt like miracles.

One of the young boys, older than me, launched the supposedly funny idea of inserting a small iron cable into an electrical outlet. He boasted that he had already done so, and that it produced a most surprising effect. Most children knew it was stupid and dangerous and ignored it. On the other hand, a young adventurer, I was on the lookout for experiments, any one. I immediately started looking for a piece of iron and quickly found a nail thin enough to fit into a socket.

I absolutely wanted to go to the end, once at home I waited until my sister was outside and I ran straight to the electrical outlet to introduce the nail, BAM! Everything happened very quickly, a powerful electric flow passed through my body right through, what an unpleasant feeling! I trembled like a leaf under the flurry and dropped the nail on the spot with a loud cry.

I ran outside to find my sister, and explained everything to her. There was still a problem, the nail had remained in the socket, there was no question of touching it again. We had the bright idea of taking a wooden broom to dislodge the nail from a distance, holding it in pairs, the little nail fell. We didn't say anything to my aunt. A few years later, in physics, I had no trouble understanding that the human body is a perfect electrical conductor.

I liked playing more than anything, even when there were no children around, I played alone. I remember one particular day, it was noon and I had just returned from my school morning in kindergarten. It was a beautiful sunny day, I was wearing a little white shirt, sitting in front of the kitchen which was outside, I was playing by pouring water from one cup to another, I found it hypnotic and entertaining, then a pointed tile came off the roof and fell right in the middle of my head.

The kitchen was covered with tiles that had just fallen, and one of them literally cracked my head.

This time, everyone thought that I would not survive. Blood rushed from my head to my little white shirt and I lost consciousness. I was lucky that my aunt came home for her break and drove me straight to the hospital. They shaved my head to put a bandage on me, and after a few days I got out of the hospital.

At that time, I had not yet left my dear province, except during the episode of the genocide. My sister had left several times, she would soon finish high school and often went to Kigali to visit my other aunts. I was looking forward to going to the capital too one day. Sometimes cars from the hospital went there and we could reserve a free place. I absolutely wanted to leave with my sister, and then who would have let a child travel without her family. That day, I heard that she had planned to leave for Kigali. Having already tried several times without success that she agrees to bring me with her, I decided to proceed in my own way.

That morning, when I was sent to borrow the iron from the neighbor's house, I hurriedly ironed my dress before bringing it back. On the way to the neighbor, I was in such a hurry that the hot iron accidentally touched the right side of my calf, I hardly felt anything at the time, and I continued walking. When I got home, I didn't feel bad at all, but I felt that my skin was getting hot. I put on my dress in fourth gear and filled a small bag with a few things that I gave to my sister. The car arrived and by the time my sister put her things in the trunk I snuck between people to sit in the car. Nobody had noticed anything. They must have thought it was agreed that I should come with them. Suddenly, a woman exclaimed near my sister: "Ah, I didn't know that your little sister was coming with you! Surprised, my sister asked me to go out, I balked vehemently. They noticed the burn on my calf and forced me to go for treatment. I finally gave in to the pressure, and I left the vehicle crying. The burn had formed a sore that quickly became infected and I ended up with a large scar on my calf.

Despite all these repetitive blunders and accidents, I still found my smile playing with my neighbors. One of them had adopted an adorable little dog that he named Bella, she loved coming to play with us in the garden. We shared a huge garden with our neighbor, a widow whose two youngest girls were the same age as me.

Under the radiant sky, we were all sitting on the garden lawn in the shade of the young trees when Bella appeared. She frightened me a bit and since I was not used to approaching her, I preferred to run away. Bella understood the opposite, certainly thinking, "Finally! A little action thanks to this sporty girl. And ran after me. Frightened, I redoubled speed to escape her, which became for Bella more and more amusing, and madly exciting. She turned on the turbo, I plunged into a heap of bushes. The dog was gone. Lying still, I remembered that something had touched me, but the adrenaline had been stronger.

I had grazed at high speed a tree with sharp branches. One of them savagely cut my cheek a few millimeters from my right eye, another miracle. My cheek was practically open, back to the hospital, the proximity of which was a boon for the smooth running of my youth. I came home with a huge bandage and I had to be treated until completely healed for several weeks. I still wear this 24 year old scar, one of many that bear witness to my dissipated youth.

We walked together every day with the neighbors' children to go to the primary school in Kilinda. There were too many of us, there was a class that started in the morning and a class in the afternoon, and vice versa the next day. The teacher had great difficulty controlling such a large number of students.

In my class, there was a very stubborn little boy Albert, almost as much as me, who enjoyed martyring me. Each time the teacher went out, he took the opportunity to hit me. It was a fight as soon as the opportunity arose, and it lasted all year without any real reason. Thank goodness we were split into two different classes in the second year. Strangely, there were far fewer of us in the third year. It was only in the fourth year that the lessons lasted all day.

At the end of my first year of elementary school, my sister had just finished her nursing studies and was going to start working at Kilinda hospital. Long before we celebrated graduation, we had moved to a larger house with three bedrooms and a garden. It was located next to the large Kilinda market. At first, I didn't like this place very much, I didn't know any local children, and then I got used to it. The market was every Monday and Thursday, and during those days you could barely pass the street.

The most annoying thing was to think of closing all the doors during the day, as many people working in the market came around tirelessly to ask for drinking water.

CARD GAMES

On market-free days, the square was nothing more than a completely empty space that we transformed into a huge playground. School holidays were the perfect time for that, all the children who lived around the market joined it to play hide and seek for whole afternoons. The vastness of the place made the game exciting, and uncontrollable. The possibilities were endless, such as changing hiding places from tree to tree depending on the researcher's placement. Some loved to show off, just to prove that they could run faster than the researcher when the researcher chased them. They ran with all their might without looking ahead, ignoring the many dangerous stones and pieces of tree trunks strewn on the ground.

One of the teachers from our primary school lived alone near us, in a large house surrounded by many guavas whose fruit was forbidden to us. The trees were saturated with guavas that the professor never picked, letting them fall to the ground and rot.

One day when he was absent, a young girl with a bad reputation offered to go and do some picking. After taking a large amount, she thought of going back to the teacher's house, and I followed her. For all this time, my aunt, who had seen me leave with this young girl, had been watching us, watching us through the fence of our house which overlooked that of the professor. When I returned, I was punished so long that the idea of going to rob guavas never touched my mind again.

Another neighbor with whom I spent a lot of time lived with her little sister in her twenties. Her 17-year-old son lived with family members in Kigali to attend secondary school. During the long holidays, he returned to spend two or three weeks with his mother. There were few young people his age in our neighborhood and he was bored. He was a reserved boy, who liked to play cards. I, who could not afford to pay for a deck of cards, came to play with him during my free time provided that he was the one who bought it. We played all day, every day until the game was completely worn out, I got a taste for cards, I was bitten. Then he bought another set of cards, which lasted until the end of the holidays.

When he left, I kept the game, and there was no one to play with until next year. Two years passed in this way, and the following year I was able to find other game partners. That summer I went to see him the day he came back and he immediately asked me if I still had the card game of the year before so we could play a game. I had the cards in my pocket, they were damaged because I had been playing all year with them and I did not dare to take them out, I replied: "No, I have no more cards".

He assured me that he would buy a new one and we left happy. Instead of taking the classic path to my home, I had the brilliant idea of choosing a shortcut that I used to take, which consisted of climbing a sloping surface that served as a fence to their house. As I leaned over, the old cards fell from my pocket and spread out before his eyes. I feel terribly ridiculous, he picked up the cards and holding them out to me at the same time as his gaze said to me, "Here, here are your cards". The next day, however, He bought a new deck of cards which was the last until we moved.

We found the old lands of my parents to exploit, the house was larger, but the rental price higher. After the genocide, we had moved for the first time because we were the only ones on this hill surrounded by destroyed houses, most of our former neighbors had perished, and the smallest detail reminded us of the tragedy. Besides, the hospital where my aunt worked was too far away. After a few years, the state financed a project to rebuild remote villages so that the inhabitants returned to live there. It was not luxury, but those who could have always had the choice of doing additional work.

This initiative which incited the people to meet had allowed the state to install common infrastructures such as drinking water, electricity and roads. My aunt had chosen one of her houses, built a fence and a kitchen there. We were few neighbors at the beginning, then the inhabitants multiplied and the houses increased in value. We have never regretted this choice. There was only one fault, my aunt and I had to travel a long distance, she to go to work, me to go to school. I was the only member of the family still in primary school, my older cousin had just failed the state exam and had landed in a private school. We never understood why she had failed, she who was so intelligent. It's not easy to walk more than forty minutes each day to go to primary school. I didn't want to change schools in the middle of the year, and it was the best school available.

To make the way with my neighbors of the same age was

impossible because they were going to a different school, we only saw each other for the end of term exams which consisted of an artistic test where we had to weave a traditional carpet, composed of long grasses to be picked near streams. We then dried them and wove everything with dried banana peels. The more careful and inventive the weaving, the higher the score. What mattered most was the size of the carpet, which had to be as large as possible.

Mine was often one of the smallest, but I did my best to keep its lines straight. There was a nifty option of waiting for a finished rug from another class to receive your grade to buy it and show it to your teacher. We preferred to build our carpets together, it was the

only school activity that I shared with my neighbors.

I was getting used to this new life, surrounded by widows and their children. My two other cousins were in high school and boarding school, I lived alone with my aunt. The state had set up a Fund (FARG) from which we benefit to pay for the studies of genocide survivors deprived of family.

It was during this period that I lost my paternal grandmother. She had moved to the area recently because the loneliness of the mountain was no longer bearable. In my spare time, I often went to her house. She was the most hygienic and sophisticated woman I had ever known. Even at her advanced age, she still took good care of herself. Hospitalized at Kilinda Hospital for several days, I remember going to see her often. They never knew what she was suffering from, they had put little pipes in her nose to help her breathe. Weakened, I can still see her greet me with her little voice: "Hello, my child's child. She always called us that, never by our first names, quite simply the children of her child. I was hoping that she would heal and go home.

My younger aunt had remarried and no longer lived with her, my grandmother lived with the son of her niece who looked after her cows and helped him on a daily basis. One afternoon, my aunt came home to tell me the bad news, grandmother had passed away. His body will be brought back to his home, and I was to stay with us while we organized everything for the funeral. It was also necessary to place an announcement on the radio so that people who knew grandmother and did not live in the region could say goodbye to her. Announcements of deceased persons appeared every morning on radio Rwanda.

I was alone all afternoon, overcome by a mixed feeling. I understood that I was no longer going to see grandmother, but with all the people I had already lost, I had become almost insensitive to death. I did not cry once. When evening fell, I slept alone while the adults watched over the fire to say goodbye. In the early morning, I got ready to go to the funeral next to her house, my cousins were there too. In the village, when a person dies, one designates a child of his family to bury him, the tradition specifies that the child should not be the elder and that he cannot bury more than one person in his life . This child is the one who throws the earth first on the coffin of the deceased and the one who pushes the cross into the earth. I was the designated child. Although I loved my grandmother very much, this choice displeased me. I was afraid she would come back to haunt me. Against my will, I accepted.

Before the burial, each went in turn to the deceased's room to say goodbye, I was told that the coffin would be closed soon, but I still didn't want to hear anything, I didn't want to see anyone anymore deceased, I had seen enough in 1994, but their arguments finally convinced me. If I didn't go see Grandma's deceased body, I would never grieve like I did with my father. I had never seen my father's dead body.

Deep inside, I was hoping it was just a huge misunderstanding, that there was always a chance that the killers were wrong, or that they had left him for dead and that he had recovered from his wounds, saved in extremis by a good Samaritan. I had imagined all kinds of scenarios, I often dreamed of seeing him come back home, alive and in great shape, telling us that he had gone far to change his identity, that he apologized that it had took so long. I finally decided to go say goodbye to my grandmother. I finally realized that no one would tell me old stories, or teach me age-old expressions.

I entered the room, my grandmother was covered in white clothes and I could only see the upper part of her face. I felt that she no longer belonged to our world. I went out, then a few minutes later everyone went to the grave and we buried her. It was the end of the grandparent's era for me, she had been my only grandmother. I regretted not having spent more time with her, not having asked her to tell me more old tales.

OUR GARDEN AND ITS ANIMALS

In the garden surrounding our house, bananas were planted to the southwest and vegetables to the east. The grass and its flowers, the space of which was dedicated to me, were located to the north in front of the entrance to the living room. The grass portion was larger than that of the flowers, which included roses and two other types of flowers that looked more like trees and withstood the dry season better. I prohibited anyone from walking in this space. This unconditional love I had for my little garden was frowned upon by my cousins who were well aware that I was giving up my share of the chores to take care of my garden. I was often told: "Flowers cannot be eaten!" Which was meant to make me realize that there were more important things to take care of.

These remarks came to my mind. I went to visit my sister who lived in a shared apartment with other young nurses in a house located in the hospital where they worked. I spent my day rummaging through her wardrobe and listening to songs on a large radio she had in her bedroom, trying to write the lyrics of the songs on a sheet of paper without even understanding the language. What fascinated me most about this place was the gardens in the hospital. They were made up of a multitude of flowers in a variety of colors and shapes, and the whole formed a magnificent floral picture. I was in love with these gardens, I did not understand how we could find and plant so many flowers so charming.

One of the roommates explained to me that seeds had been planted there and that the flowers grew from those seeds. She promised to give me seeds next season when I come back to visit them. I returned to Rusenge, cherishing this promise, lulled by the vision of my future little garden filled with soon flourishing seeds. My imagination had no limits and I told anyone who wanted to hear that I had the serious project of planting a whole field of flowers to take it to Europe. It made everyone laugh a lot, I was often told: "Good idea! " Flowers were the great passion of my childhood.

A colleague and neighbor of my aunt owned a very cute little black cat with green eyes. I had been sent to her home to send her a message when in the middle of our conversation, her cat passed by us. I remembered at that time that we had a mouse at home and that my aunt said that one day, we would borrow the cat from the neighbor for a few days, that would be enough for the mice to be afraid and never come back again . I immediately announced, "Aunty also told me to ask you if you would agree to lend us your cat for a few days to scare the mice? " She agreed and I took the cat with me. We were already fortunate to have cows, and now a cat to give milk to, I spent so much time playing with it. Then the day came when we had to return the cat.

I would miss her a lot but I had no choice, I brought her back to her owner, less than a kilometer from us.

The same evening, we heard the cat meowing and scratching at our door, he had found the way all alone. We brought her back to her owner several times but he still managed to come back. Finally, its owner decided to give it to us and he became my cat. Since it was a female, I gave her the name of Duchesse, as in the book from my early childhood.

When family friends came to visit us, they often left me ten, twenty, fifty or even one hundred Rwandan franc banknotes for me to buy candy or cookies. Instead of spending all this money, I placed all my coins in a pot, one day reaching the sum of 1500 Rwandan Francs. I invested this amount in the purchase of a hen, which in a fairly short period of time gave us chicks. The chicks grew, reproduced and I ended up with dozens of hens. My aunt had a larger cage built to accommodate them in the garden. Among the growing chicks were also roosters, but no more than one could be kept. Once they were big, I sold them. My small business worked so well that one day I sold everything for a goat, although this animal reproduces less quickly than a chicken.

There were not always only domestic animals around us. Some rumors, which were rather an extension of urban legends, circulated about the presence around wild animals. We heard most often about the hyenas but never got any evidence. What was not a rumor was the strong presence of snakes, the majority of which were very poisonous. When you saw the moulting skin of a snake, you had to keep in mind that it could be around. We didn't see it every day, but we had all seen at least one. Our house had a wooden fence around which I had planted a Maracuja tree so that its lianas embrace the fence and give it a more lively and full appearance. You could pick fruit there in the summer and this leafy fence could be a perfect hideout for snakes.

One day when I and my cousins were in the outdoor kitchen, one of them went to look for something in the house. Suddenly she heard a loud cry of fear. We rushed to find in the small hallway of the entrance, a green and shiny snake of medium size, to crawl with difficulty.

If he had had time to cross the yard, he was now stuck in the rough, cemented corridor that kept him from sliding. We were far too petrified to act, our only reaction was to run outside and cry out for help.

Without delay, men from the neighborhood rushed to molest the snake to death.

The summer is favorable with this kind of meeting, because of the heat, the snakes leave their holes in the hope of drinking. At certain very hot hours of the day, it was always oppressive for the mind to walk around the bushes. One day when I was passing by a narrow dirt road, I heard whistles. I was very scared, not knowing where it came from, I just wanted to move fast to get to a bigger road. It could have come from anywhere, and then about five meters from me, I saw a very large golden-skinned snake crossing the small path at high speed. Static, I watched him without even breathing so he wouldn't hear me. His waist was disconcerting, about 35 to 40 cm and it was immensely long. I must have waited a moment before seeing the tail of this horrible thing slide definitively on the other side, down this little alley where a stream flowed.

When the end of this thing disappeared I started to run to the main road. I could not believe my eyes. I was very scared and at the same time I was fascinated, the incredible nature had still dazzled me by its excess and its beauty. The climate of Rwanda favors the development of certain species which are not all as pleasant as one would like.

The caterpillars that grow in our region, for example, are black, hairy, with a red head, and can be found in any green space. I have been their victim twice, they just have to move on your skin to plant hairs everywhere in its path. Very short and painful hairs which are practically impossible to extract. One of them had managed to hide in a sheet that had been left to dry on the grass and that same evening, I was sleeping in these sheets.

The next morning I noticed with amazement that I had swollen skin in several places. The caterpillar had had time to cover a long distance on my skin when I saw it continue on its way on my bed.

The moment arrived when I had to go to boarding school for my secondary studies. I sold my goat and kept the money, my little business was over. My grades were pretty good, unfortunately at the end of the sixth year of primary school, I just missed the exam that would have allowed me to go to the best secondary school in the state. State aid covered my school fees, so I was sent to a private school boarding school. For a young girl like me, used to living alone with her aunt, the first year was not easy. I had to get used to the operation of a school where discipline was not the priority.

The facility was known to accommodate all lost and unmotivated children in the area, and the success rate there was clearly lower than elsewhere. The classes, the administration, the refectory and a large part of the dormitories were in the same place, enclosed by a single gate, which was watched daily by a guard. The first and fourth years were assigned to the external dormitories, and for some strange reason, I and a few other beginners were placed in the internal dormitories for a few weeks. I didn't like being mixed up with older students. Fortunately, we ended up giving us a place in the external dormitories, the buildings were new and larger. It was then that I was able to make new friends. I quickly adapted to the lessons and succeeded rather well despite my chaotic pedigree. My favorite lesson was the music lesson. I was doing so well that I thought I could have a career as a pianist, and I sang the notes as if they came to me, much better than all the others. Unfortunately, this school did not offer a serious music option because the profession of musician was little considered, given the prevailing sciences and languages.

The food offered at the boarding school was not really to my liking, but when we had an exit permit, I was lucky to be able to go to my sister's house to eat.

Getting used to the lifestyle offered by this school was a real challenge. There wasn't always enough food for everyone. For fussy stomachs, eating the same thing every day was less than ideal. There was also a small canteen which was next to the gate, we would spend our pocket money in addition to other needs such as soap and toothpaste. We didn't all have the same financial means, the better-off went more often, and some did not go at all. For my part, I was lucky to be able to spend a little there. This extra canteen offered milk tea for the morning which cost fifty Rwandan francs, milk donuts which cost a little more, as well as many other little things like fruit and cookies. You had to go to bed late to review and get up very early to be on time in class. Every morning when I woke up, I dreamed of the day when I would finally finish my studies.

HOLIDAYS

For holidays, I almost always came home, I also sometimes went to visit my cousins who lived in the capital. It was very different from the village, I discovered a lot there. My cousins were more connected than me and led an intense city life. Although I loved going there, I quickly missed my little campaign. I felt much more free in nature, while in town life seemed too modern and excessive, my mind was suffocating. We watched a lot of television, I was impressed by the multitude of TV shows, musical films, and many other things. All that I had known about media culture before was a few photo novels that my cousins had brought back to the village. Our only television channel was the national TVR, whose broadcasting rules were strict. When there was a scene where two people were kissing, the images were censored by the national flag. The city remained fascinating, in my small village, I had grown up without electricity, and my cousins from Kigali brought me once a year the clothes that no longer suited them. I loved it, they were trendy and in a style we didn't know. The capital was superb, but it was hard to get around because the places looked so much alike. My cousin's life seemed easy to me, they didn't have to take care of the cows or the land, they had time to go play football, see friends or watch TV. This new world made me fantasize.

When I was vacationing at home, my priority was to rest to recover from the fatigue of a long term spent studying tirelessly. At the time of my secondary studies, we no longer had any domestic help because my aunt considered that it was no longer necessary. Until now, I had never needed to do many things at home, especially when it came to household chores and cooking.

When it wasn't our housekeeper who did it, it was my cousins. I don't know why, but they always did everything for me, maybe it was because they hoped to ease the trauma of the genocide by making my life easier.

This vacation was a breath of fresh air. The course of a typical day started with a classic breakfast, then I went to keep the cows, especially in summer. In Rwanda, cows never stayed on fenced pasture, unless the herd was large. They were generally walked from field to field depending on the quality or freshness of the herbs available. I often met other children in the village with their cows, we put the ruminants together and we spent our days having fun.

When we find a banana tree accidentally dropped, we take the opportunity to hide the raw bananas in a warm place. The ideal was to dig and wrap the bananas in peels to bury them and then come back a few days later to eat them. The process was the same for avocados. There are many avocado trees in the Rwandan forests, it often happened that many avocados fell, and sometimes on our heads. The only thing that mattered was counting the days to know when the avocados or bananas were ripe.

The most exciting time was the summer holidays, harvest season, and especially sorghum, a plant with many attributes. When harvested, the bark can be used as food for the cows and the sorghum grains are brought home. We leave them outside for several days until they are dry, then we hit them to drop the seeds that we collect. From this moment, the sorghum is ready to be consumed, we can for example make porridge for a very nutritious breakfast. Before that, you have to take the seeds to the mill to make flour. Before modern mills arrived, you had to crush them yourself using a traditional mill made up of two stones: one thicker and thicker and the other fine. From the porridge, it could be transformed into a summer drink, or as brewer's yeast called "Urwagwa".

It was in the sorghum fields that we often brought the cows in summer. Barefoot, you had to be careful with the floor, which was difficult to walk on and painful. You could quickly end up with a cut under the arch. In summer, the ground was so hard as stone that you could dig a so-called "Runonko" oven. Once it was finished, very fine wood was placed there for the fire, adding small logs until the temperature increased, then baking a few sweet potatoes.

Once filled, the hot oven was crushed on the sweet potatoes, which were trapped in the sweltering heat. After a few tens of minutes, the sweet potatoes were eaten directly on the spot.

After my first long summer holiday, I found a new school for my second year. Catholic schools were considered more serious, whether private or public. It was still not a state school but it was already an improvement. To have the chance to join a state school along the way, you had to either be an excellent sportsman, or be trained by a high-ranking person. So I joined the Immaculate Conception College run by the good sisters of the "Benebikira" congregation. A school located in Butare, region which saw the birth of the first National University of Rwanda which had its own hospital.

Most of our teachers were students in their final year of university. We were very well trained and the operation of the school was rigorous. This region of Save, where our establishment was located, had three other secondary schools belonging to religious or state brothers. It was a small area made up mostly of schools and its boarding school campuses.

About a hundred yards from our school was an antediluvian church. Every morning at dawn, we revise for two hours before having breakfast. Then when the time for the morning mass struck, everyone could choose to go there or not. On Thursdays and Sundays, however, mass was compulsory for all. Every Thursday, our school sang, and each class had its turn. It was absolutely necessary to go to the song rehearsals and on Sundays, a church choir gave a high performance. Although I was not a Catholic, I felt closer and closer to this religion. I started by coming to non-compulsory morning masses, especially to listen to one of our favorite priests who preached the gospel with admirable and bewitching fervor. Happened by his charisma, his words struck us in the heart. He was a handsome, tall-looking man, but his back was strangely hunched.

The story circulated that he had been hidden in a small wardrobe during the whole period of the genocide, and that his back had taken the form of this providential cockpit.

My real growth started, I started to select my clothes carefully and I wrote love songs. I had made several friends and everything was going well, until the fateful month of April. The common trauma of the genocide reached the weakest, and gradually reached all the other students. The boarding school favored the resurgence of the psychic wounds which rekindled annually in April. The wounds of the genocide were still present and active for many of us, and the crises were violent. It only took one student to crack to train everyone else. In April 2006 the phenomenon worsened, several students, including myself, went through a terribly long traumatic crisis that spread throughout the school.

This crisis was characterized by a wave of immense and inexplicable fear, nightmares, hallucinations, screams, dementia, which particularly affected those who were children at the time of the events. Unlike adults who knew the political situation in 1994 and who could have expected war, the children had been psychologically broke, branded by the surprise of the attacks.

In their minds remained the indelible fear that attacks could resurface at any time, for no reason.

In these moments of crisis, I wondered what I could have done wrong to deserve this. My father's alleged killer was still in prison and I had never been able to put a face on this devil, I was unconsciously looking for culprits around me. I felt a strong need to direct my hatred towards someone or something. What will never cease to amaze me is that for a long time, I resented my aunt when she was a victim as much as I was. She was the only person I knew well enough to be able to direct my frustrations there. I was totally lost, I didn't understand what reality was, I had nightmares every night, dreaming of corpses coming out of public graves to come and attack me.

I knew where these public graves were. One of them was now a skeptical pit near the house of our wealthy uncle in Kigali whom he had built for his mother, one of my grandfather's wives. This house was bordered by a small dirt road which I used every day as a shortcut to go to primary school. My stepmother had been thrown into this pit, along with everyone else who lived nearby. I thought about it every morning I went this way, and although I knew there was no body there, I was still scared. Using my backpack, I hid the right side of my face on the way out and the left side on my way back.

In one of the school dormitories, one of us just had to cry out for all of our bad memories to come back. Incessantly, we relived the same scenes, I cried out to ask for mercy and that no one kill me. I distinctly saw machetes cleaving the air in my search, I mixed my memories and those that I had been told.
Some of us who were far too agitated had to be brought under control, while most of us cried, choked or shouted, others started running as if they were being chased. Sometimes I hid under the bed, behind or anywhere, and it could last a long time. If someone from the school staff intervened, it was important that they did not touch me at the risk of causing endless screams. As the slightest intervention can be perceived as an attack, the best thing was to let the students calm down by themselves.

It was in the third year that the crises took on desperate proportions. Until then, we had been able to simply let the students rest in their dormitories, and when the crises were more severe, we would take them to Save hospital to give them sedatives. But this time, the number of sufferers had increased, the waves of the past had become more contagious than usual, the school could no longer contain us. The Save hospital being already filled, the great University hospital of Butare had to intervene.

The whole ambulance of the university hospital was still not enough. It was out of the question to leave those who were not reached in the company of people in crisis at the risk of further spreading the phenomenon. Teachers who owned vehicles therefore participated in transportation. Two young girls and I were transported to the hospital, but the additional rooms which had been furnished with mattresses on the floor were already full. The teacher who had transported us then decided to drive us to his home.

I didn't realize where I was until I woke up the next day, probably because of the effect of the painkillers. That morning his wife took care of us with all the kindness imaginable and we got to know their two adorable little children.

There was talk of transferring us to the hospital as soon as space became available, our parents had been informed of the arrangements and were awaiting further instructions. Those who had not been seized had a week's vacation to get back on their feet. We stayed at the teacher's home until the middle of the day and then taken to the hospital.

One of the girls returned home the same day, the second returned quickly enough, I was the only one who had to be taken to the hospital. Before leaving, the teacher's wife told us that she wanted to see us again if we ever went through Butare.

I was taken to the hospital where there were still a lot of students. We all felt like we were getting better, but it was only the painkillers that had softened us considerably. During these few days, I stayed in bed all day and only sat down to receive my meal. The most severe seizures occurred after dark. Once again, it was only a sound that sounded like a cry, and we all found ourselves immersed in sordid hallucinations where it was no longer possible to differentiate between past and reality. To prevent us from feeling abandoned, a few university students volunteered to come and talk to us in the early evening. They stayed with us sometimes until very late, until we all fell asleep. There was no cure, it would have taken an army of psychologists to hope that several generations of traumatized children could be cured. Students were dropping home when their parents could pick them up. For me, two provinces separated me from Butare, and to access it, you had to take a bus to reach Gitarama, on a road without macadam and difficult to pass. This same road made me throw up my guts so many times.

It is then necessary to take a connection to Gitarama to head towards Butare, from there, driving becomes easier.

The only person who could come and get me was my aunt, but coming here was an impossible undertaking. She had to ask for several days off from work, find a place to sleep once here because going back in the day was impossible, not to mention the difficulty of finding a means of transportation from our region. And even if all this became possible, even if I had been able to be in contact with her, when the phone was not installed at her place. So I took on myself, like the handful of students who stayed at the hospital that week, and we returned to the boarding school a few days later.

Classes resumed, the term went off without a hitch, and I only came home for school holidays, as usual. At the end of the vacation I left for the last trimester. I knew my propensity to miss the bus that will get me there in time, and I was now taking precautions to get there in advance. This time I arrived too far in advance, the boarding school was empty. I dropped off my things and went for a walk in Butare. I was 15 years old and started to feel independent and able to find my own way in this big city. That day, there was an event that the whole city was waiting for, a rally race, an extremely popular sport. The city was more crowded than usual and an atmosphere of excitement was felt. The roads were closed to public transportation for the purposes of the race, so I walked for a while. Suddenly I recognized the house of the teacher who had housed us during the episode of the crises. I thought that on a Sunday like this, they should certainly be at home and that he would be happy if I came to greet them.

I rang the bell and the servant came to open the door. He installed me in the living room, while waiting to warn the owners of the house. The professor came in, greeted me thanking me for saying hello, and informed me that his wife and children had gone for a walk and were soon to return. He offered me a glass of Maracuja juice which I accepted, then the servant left the room.

The professor approached me, a little too close. I was intimidated and disgusted, I had just turned 15 and this man who was sticking with me was old enough to be my father. I walked away while remaining polite, and in a split second, he literally pounced on me to stick his disgusting tongue in my mouth. It must have weighed more than 100 kilos, but I was able to gather all my strength to throw it to the ground when the noise of a car was heard. Panicked, he withdrew hastily.

It took me a good minute to realize that his wife had just arrived and that I was saved. He quickly arranged to go out to welcome his wife, who came to greet me without delay. I announced that I was in a big hurry, that I had only come to say hello. She smiled and asked me to wait a minute.

She reappeared with her wallet in hand and handed me a 1000 Rwandan franc note, explaining to me that it could serve as my return ticket, when the ticket did not exceed two hundred Rwandan Francs. I kindly thanked him by replying that I had enough money to buy a ticket, and left without taking the money. Once away from this house, I realized for the first time that you had to be wary of men.

I arrived at the boarding school in the early evening and sat on my bed to unpack my things.

There were only bunk beds, mine was at the end of the dormitory, glued to a wall, and I was lucky to have been able to choose the one at the bottom.

The student who occupied the opposite bed was in my class, she was a calm and kind girl, and we were friends. While I was unpacking my things, I asked her how she found the outfit I was wearing.

This question seemed strange to her, but she replied that it was going well, and that the outfit was beautiful. I asked her to tell me if she didn't find it provocative, and that made her laugh. I wore three-quarter jeans with red bands fashionable at the time, a long-sleeved half-white t-shirt and white sneakers on my feet. My outfit was more comfortable than anything, nothing that would encourage inappropriate behavior.

Yielding to my friend's insistent look, I told her everything. She was neither shocked nor surprised by my story. She was a girl from the capital, she may have already experienced this kind of situation. She advised me to be on my guard, and repeated several times that men are not always driven by good intentions. You have to believe that this was not going to be my only lesson on this.

At the end of the third year, I was one of the very small number of students who had passed the lower cycle exam. I was finally going to be able to go to a state school. I also had the choice to stay in this establishment for my graduate studies, I had just met my first boyfriend there. I loved him madly, our relationship was largely nourished by little love letters that we exchanged and I no longer wanted to leave this school. Through sustained arguments, and without ever revealing my real intentions, I managed to persuade my mother to let me go back.

RETURN TO KABGAYI

Only one day after the start of the school year, I already regretted not having chosen the state school and decided to leave. When I got the assignment paper, I was surprised to learn that it was the Saint-Joseph school group in Kabgayi, the same one where we had hidden during the genocide. I packed my bags and phoned my aunt so I wouldn't tell her until I got there. When the taxi approached the school, I saw a large cemetery dedicated to the victims. I couldn't help but think about how lucky I was not to be buried there. I started to cross the little road on foot that I knew well, but the landscape had changed. It was not until I passed the gate that I recognized, as if it were yesterday, the innumerable recesses that I had surveyed so much 10 years previously. We had lived in this class, there opposite the direction, near the garden where I had satiated.

I deposited the proof of my assignment with the direction which registered me and by surprise, I crossed a cousin who studied and lived in this boarding school for a year. While she was showing me around, I felt relieved because now I could count on her. I missed my boyfriend, but I quickly made new friends. The lively and warm atmosphere of the place almost made me forget the horrors that had taken place there. Sports events and competitions were highlighted, the inter-school cups won by our players were celebrated with fervor throughout the school.

I was 16 now, and that slender tomboy body was gone. The woman that I would be was taking shape, heads were starting to turn. The first week, a very good friend who studied in 5th letters came to find me to observe me, she had heard that a new student looked like me like two drops of water.

It was really my anatomical double, but it had a very bad reputation. I didn't care, she was so nice to me, she called me "little sister".

I finished the first trimester with good grades and we left for the Easter holidays. I returned to boarding school two weeks later for the second term.

I was already well integrated and sometimes went to see the girl who looked like me in her class. One day, she introduced me to a friend of hers who was in 6th grade, one of the best basketball players in the school.

I was not really interested in sports, I only attended games for the atmosphere. A few days later, I met him in front of our refectory, he looked much older compared to the other students in his class, he must have been over 25 years old. We chatted for a few minutes, he told me his name was Ivan, then the post-dinner review bell rang and I went back to my class. On that day, students who wished to do so could also return to the refectory to watch the Chelsea vs Liverpool game.

Since these two hours after meals passed slowly, some students sometimes went to sleep directly if no one noticed. There were all kinds of tricks to dry these revisions, and when the porter was in a good mood, you could go through the gate to get to the dorms. I felt tired, so I left the classroom to take a look and check that the way was clear. I stepped out and in front of my class stood Ivan, which I thought was accidental. He said he knew the porter well, that the porter would let us pass, and we went out without problems. He offered to accompany me to my dorm, the streets were dangerous at night, and Ivan knew some shortcuts where you wouldn't run into the authorities.

Where could this blind confidence come from despite my past? I followed him without asking any questions, we passed by the cemetery, which had the gift of frightening me.

We crossed the road to end up in a forest road which led to

the handball field. I started to be afraid, I regretted having followed him and having wanted to dry the reviews, we were clearly no longer on a path which led to my dormitory. No car was passing on this road, there was only darkness and that damn cemetery that separated us from the inhabited places. Ivan stopped and approached me, I was more and more afraid and I felt so naive. He pressed me against a wall of earth and pulled up my skirt. I struggled as best I could but he had a lot more strength. I tried to negotiate, begged him to do nothing and promised to find him another time in a decent place. It didn't work, he raped me. It was my first time.

I was angry and unable to find my way alone. I was mad at myself, I thought it was my fault. Ivan offered to take me back to the dorm, I had already decided that I would not say anything. Anyway, nobody would have believed me, at that time if a rape took place it was that the victim had looked for it. I followed Ivan, when we arrived the gate to the girls' dorm was closed.

I knocked and behind the closed door, the host told me to go to sleep in the school dormitories. On the way back, we met the students returning from the football match, they were shouting about Liverpool who had scored two goals against Chelsea. The host had already called the school to warn, I arrived followed by Ivan and guards were waiting for us at the entrance. I no longer knew very well where I was, everything had happened so quickly. My hair was full of dry grass and the back of my jacket was covered in mud, and they all thought they understood what had happened. Ivan came back quickly and no one said anything to him since he was an important basketball player, and they kept me.

They were angry and asked lots of questions, like it was all my fault. I denied it all, the truth would have cost me too much. I told them that I had been to see the match and that Liverpool had two goals against Chelsea.

An animator took me to her room and asked me to take off my panties. She saw the blood and I said that I practice karate and that I was hit in the crotch.

The next day, the whole school knew about it and they all ogled me out like I was a prostitute. I could hear whispering and chatting behind my back wherever I went. The pressure was such that I felt guilty, and maybe it was.

I had no more friends, my cousin came to speak to me brutally and made me understand that I made her ashamed. I was very afraid of being fired, the same morning the basketball coach advised Ivan to leave and sent his players to tell me precisely the facts that I will have to tell in order not to be fired. The only thing that interested them was to preserve Ivan and not me. They wanted me to admit everything to the management, then they changed their minds. In any case, Ivan will stay and it will be my fault. In the evening, my supposed twin came to see me, spoke to me kindly, assured me that what had happened did not matter, and that she understood me. She advised me to go to the chapel and to quote this prayer: "Lord, do not abandon me, remember that I am your child, if I got lost, help me to get back on the right path, amen" .

After the evening meal, I went to the chapel, recited the prayer and I cried, a lot. I felt relieved and went to the reviews. The next day, the director brother called me into his office and asked me a long series of questions. This interrogation was a real torture, he wanted to know everything that had happened to the last detail. Why was it necessary?

I was already aware of the conclusions of their meetings about me: I was a nuisance for everyone. I was nobody, and Ivan was their favorite player. I did not talk about rape, and I always kept to my version of karate player. Before leaving his office, after he asked me to confirm that I was still a virgin, I knelt at his feet and begged him to forgive me, repeating that I did not want to be fired, that I had always been a reasonable person, overwhelmed by this catastrophic situation.

My greatest wish was to be able to go back in time to erase this episode from my life. I was a minor, they should have informed the police. The prefect of studies wanted to send Ivan to prison and they found the arguments to dissuade him.

Even if I felt more and more guilty, what could I have said to the police? The customs of that time did not make much of rape. I have buried my sadness and bitterness deep inside me, and the anxieties of the past have resurfaced. I would have loved so much that my father was still alive to defend his little girl.

How could so many painful injustices happen to one person? My self-esteem broke down, I could no longer see the bright side of life. I got up painfully every morning and spent my day like an ectoplasm, unable to bear the shock. When was it going to end?

Will there be hope for a better future? I did not let any emotion show through and this further fueled the students' conversations: "Look how she doesn't care, she probably used to do that".

Some time later, one of my aunt's daughters came by unexpectedly to say hello. She had stopped on her way from Rusenge to Kigali where she was studying at university. We chatted outside the portal and no one knew she had come. Normally, visits were prohibited, except on the first Sunday of the month. Life in boarding school was not easy, we were all eager for any visit, synonymous with pocket money.

As a former pupil of the establishment, she knew the procedure and melted into the crowd to pass the gate without the porter knowing it. In other circumstances, this visit would have been a pleasant surprise, but that day, I was afraid that she would hear the bad news. The students were watching us, and my cousin probably couldn't understand why. She obviously didn't know why I was the star of the school. We chatted on banalities, laughed a lot and I didn't say anything about what I was going through, then after an hour she left.

The student dorms were inside the school, except for the first and fourth years who lived nearby. Regarding the glorious student players, they slept in reserved and equipped dormitories inside the school.

I had long and until exhaustion tried to understand how my incident had been able to go around the school in the space of half a day, and I had resolved myself to the idea that it would not be useful to me. anyway to nothing. A good comrade and excellent volleyball player named Bienvenu was the one who told me the truth. When Ivan returned that night to the players' dormitory, he woke up his colleagues to say that he had made a daughter for himself. He was so proud to have pawned the other players who were chasing me. The next morning, the whole school knew about it.

The next day, my mental state got worse, I wanted to end it. I left school in the early afternoon to head for the side of the road which had a steep slope. The cars had very little visibility. This ride has been etched in my memory forever. I was specially dressed in my white uniform shirt, a khaki uniform skirt, and my white asics sneakers bought a year ago at the Shyembe market near Rusenge. My outfit was impeccable, and was my only comfort. It was a sunny and warm day, the street was empty.

I had planned to kill myself by throwing myself in front of the first car that would arrive at high speed, I was no longer able to live that way.

There was very little traffic and for some reason I still don't have the courage to do so. I watched the few cars pass and went back to the school.

My cousin had hidden from me that I had given my aunt's number to the school administration. One Saturday morning when we were all idle, except for the teams that were training, this director's word mill passed by me and said, "You really look like your aunt." I immediately understood what was going on. They decided to fire me, and called her to take me home. Except that when she got to school, she lost her temper because she knew she couldn't find any other school that would accept a girl after such a dismissal. They took pity on her, and did not dismiss me, I later learned that was the only reason.

Immediately after learning of my aunt's presence, I left the dorms to hide in a small room that once had been used as a goat stable. My aunt, the director and my cousin started looking for me everywhere. Then all the students joined them, as well as the girl I looked like, who once in the stable saw me hidden behind the door. Struck by my panicked face, she came out saying she hadn't seen anything. When they gave up the search, I felt guilty thinking of my poor aunt who was going to make the round trip for nothing.

I decided to get out of my hiding place and I showed up. They took me away from the eyes of the other students, I feared the torture of the interrogation, had I not been humiliated enough?

I simulated a passing out, dropped to the floor, and played unconscious for several minutes. Survival strategy. I was starting to understand that you could only count on yourself and I became a strong teenager. My aunt wanted me to tell her what had happened but I did not want to discuss it any more, besides I had not finally told the truth to anyone. None of them deserved me to open my heart to them, they all decided the script in advance and spread it.

My aunt left, and that reputation stuck with me for the next two years. Ivan returned to school as if nothing had happened, and continued his career as a revered school player.

NOT QUITE DEAD

Every year between April 7 and 14, the country goes through a week of national mourning. Sad songs are played on radio and television, as well as testimonies from some survivors of the genocide. As I said earlier, this is a good time for post-trauma crises. On the last day of mourning, the inhabitants gather at the feet of the nearest monument where the victims of the genocide rest and perform a ceremony in their honor. I participated in these ceremonies every year when my father was not buried in any of these monuments, his body having never been found.

One of my father's murderers was a neighbor, before the war my father had offered him work several times. My father was captured by Igitero, a group of killers armed with machetes. I never really cried my father because I never saw him dead. I was in denial and still hoped he would come back someday.

What I do know is that one of my sisters cried a lot when they heard the detailed story of the capture and execution of our father, the nice man from the village.

He was captured about 500 meters from the village, and knocked out with a machete in the neck. He collapsed on the ground in the middle of the road. The Interahamwe gloated at the sight of his blood spurting and spilling on the road which remained marked for several months after.

His blood was flowing, but he was not quite dead. They let him die and left. For several days, he survived without being able to move while waiting for someone to come and rescue him, then he died. I can't imagine how much he could have suffered. One of the residents found that the show had lasted long enough, and pulled the body to a forest below to bury it.

We never could find out where. Had he checked if he was

alive? Did he care that there was still an ounce of vitality in this body? This is what I keep thinking about.

This neighbor was imprisoned after the testimonies of the other killers who denounced him for several crimes. Given the large number of people indicted, the state organized in 2005 the Gacaca courts which is pronounced "Gatchatcha", a community village court which made it possible to speed up the trials.

Originally, the Gacaca made it possible to settle neighborhood or family conflicts on the hills, whose customs were far removed from modern judicial practices. It was a village assembly chaired by elders where everyone could ask to speak.

Gacaca means "sweet grass", that is the place where we meet. It was stipulated that if the accused admitted his crime, offered a sincere apology to the victims and denounced his accomplices, he could hope to see his sentence reduced by counting the years already spent. My father's killer fulfilled all of these conditions and was released. He lived by the side of the road, I often saw him come out of his little house when I passed by. He looked down and wondered how this miserable man had the courage to commit such atrocious crimes. I had already forgiven him. From a very young age, I did not feel any bitterness towards the murderers, perhaps because I could not conceive of such acts. It could be a form of denial, by becoming aware of the situation, I told myself that it was useless to hold a grudge, it was necessary to do justice and nothing else was useful. I had empathy for the tormented minds of the killers in the grip of terrible suffering, I had forgiven them everything.

They insisted and asked the killer several times where my father's body was. He showed us a place in a forest which was at the bottom of the road on a sloping surface. Men from the village dug in several places without success until exhaustion. A few days later, he designated another place, but nothing was found. After having designated more than 4 places without finding anything there, we abandoned the search. Perhaps it had been picked up after the war and buried in the mass or else scavengers had eaten it. We felt like we had been wandering around like in an unhealthy game, but thinking about it, after all this frenzy of thousands of murders, which could remember the location of a single man years later.

In 2007, I was in boarding school for the second quarter of my fifth year. We were in the second half of April and winter was raging. The owner of the patch of forest where we had dug repeatedly came to alert us to a find. Because of the heavy rains, the sloping ground had been washed away by the floods which had exposed the roots of the trees. A human arm bone protruded from the ground. It was the same forest but the place was quite far from the locations designated by the killer.

A team of men from the village came to dig and found the rest of the body in his almost intact clothes he was wearing before he left us. It was elephant-paste jeans pants and a yellow, blue and red check shirt. Some buttons were still fixed and those of the jeans had rusted. They left his body at the town hall while waiting for the summer vacation so that we could take it together to the war memorial.

The holidays finally arrived, and it was when I got home that I heard the news. It made me feel a pinch, even though I knew that my father was dead, that his killer had confessed, I had always kept the tiny hope that all this could be false, that he had made the wrong victim and that one day my father would come home.

This news destroyed the last bit of dream and miracle, of all hope in me. I already had an emotional, sad shell and did not cry. Together, we made an appointment at the town hall office.

An empty room was reserved for my father's body. When we entered, there was a big bag next to a bench that contained his bones. Windows without curtains made the room bright. It was a Sunday and the other offices were all closed, silence reigned.

We sat on the bench, I felt a really strange feeling, how could a person I had loved so much end up in this black bag? I wanted to talk to him but I was afraid of looking ridiculous, after all it was no longer my father.

One of us went out to get basins of water for cleaning. We opened the bag full of messy bones, the top of the pants were still on the bones of the pelvis, and other pieces of clothing were mixed in the pile. Most of the shirt buttons were still hanging from their buttonholes. We had already seen many body bones during the ceremonies, and those of our father did not shock us.

We washed each bone, we had to do it together for the mourning to be complete. The silence was heavy, no one spoke. There was nothing more to say. After that, we could look ahead and live our lives with the gratitude that we were fortunate enough to survive. We were told one day that my father always wanted to die before my aunts because he knew they would take care of us better than he could have done, he had foreseen the arrival of the genocide.

While we were washing his bones, I noticed a button on his shirt that had come off and I slipped it into my pocket without anyone noticing. We were going to bury him in a public monument, I had the right to keep a small memory of him.

Once everything was clean and spread on the bag to be able to dry, we cleaned the basins, then we said goodbye and went home.

Some time later, we organized a farewell ceremony at the nearest war memorial where several people came to support us. There was little crying, time had done its work. We were relieved that he was buried with dignity and rested in peace.

I returned to boarding school at the end of the vacation, the third trimester went pretty well. The Gacaca had proven to be saving and useful for the country but we did not really feel safe with all these former killers in the wild. Some supported by their families allowed themselves to put pressure on survivors to prevent them from testifying against them. We quickly received similar threats.

A talented Rwandan singer composed a song in which he recounted what his native region had experienced during the massacres. During the week of commemoration in April, this song was played several times on the radio, the singer cited some names of people the region had lost.

This song aroused a lot of emotions in some people, and this is how survivors from other regions began to collect money to pay the singer and finance other songs to pay tribute to members of their missing family or friends. It was around 2013 that in Kilinda, we finally got our homage song. My father's name was mentioned there, as well as other people who lived around the hospital. One of them was a renowned doctor who had worked there for many years. This man had not been killed in an ordinary way, the tortures which the killers had inflicted on him amounted to torture. After opening his stomach, he was forced to cite the name of each organ that the killers had extirpated. It seems that the poor man would have cited almost all of them until they died. Among the killers were former doctors' patients.

At the end of my school year, a former military uncle took me to Europe so that I could try my luck. He was one of our surviving maternal uncles who had left long ago. He had the financial means to offer me a plane ticket, and we went to visit his many acquaintances, friendly families and people my age. There, I felt safe and everyone treated me like a normal person.

EUROPE

Destination Belgium, where the newly acquired majority gave me the right to live there alone. I had read a lot of photo novels and seen TV shows that talked about Europe, but the reality was much more impressive. The tall buildings that overwhelm you with their immensity, all these endless miraculous lights that sparkle and above all, all these whites, everywhere. In my childhood, the few white people I saw in real life were those who came to work in hospitals and schools for NGOs after the war. The most comforting was the feeling of security. Nobody knew me, I could start all over again.

My priority was to get back to school quickly, but 18 was too old to enroll in high school. The only remaining option was to integrate a remedial diploma program called social advancement which was enrolled over two school years and which led to the presentation of an end of study assignment, with the secondary school diploma at the end.

Arriving in February and impatient, I hardly waited six months before I could start the school year.

Although I had taken French lessons in Rwanda, and all my notes had been taken in French, I had great difficulty understanding the spoken European accent. In truth, I nodded out of politeness and timidity, because most of the time I did not understand anything at all what I was told, ditto for writing. Thanks to TV, I gradually got used to the local specificities of the language. Since I had not followed my primary studies in Belgium, it was necessary that one month before the start of the school year, I passed admissions tests to enter social advancement. This exam included: a math test, French and English, validated hands down.

A little later, I was a student and lived in a studio on the fifth floor of a building near the center of Liège, in Wallonia.

To finance the equipment of my small apartment, I worked weekends and two days a week as a coffee waitress in the center. I used to work whole evenings. This pace didn't bother me on weekends but on weekdays, I came home and took a quick shower to go straight to class.

My first weeks in class were difficult. I only integrated one concept out of three and dared not speak. I still had pronunciation and articulation difficulties. When I had to speak, panic swept over me and I became the dumb 5-year-old girl again until Jesus returned. The simple idea of having to speak in class petrified me.

I had no classmates, I dared not go to them and no one came to me. I must have looked like a country girl, I was not invited to student evenings. I still managed to make some friends among the work colleagues at the cafe. We went out from time to time, unfortunately the best days to go out were those where I worked and I did all the slots that nobody wanted, Christmas, New Year, ... it allowed me to have some money aside, which I largely sent to my family in Rwanda.

Very determined to get out of it, that same year I got a summer job in a hotel in the North Sea. It was completely new to me but I wanted to try it out. The hotel was crowded with tourists, I had to serve breakfast and then clean the rooms. I did everything wrong and I was always clumsy in front of clients. I was dismissed after a few days. My roommate informed me that there was a free place in a large restaurant to take the plunge. She advised me: "Be quick and efficient. I introduced myself and the boss hired me immediately.

I did not fail to put into practice the advice of my roommate and in just a few hours it worked wonderfully, everyone was happy with me.

I was fired for the second time, the owner realized that I did not have a work permit, I was not aware that I needed one. I was able to finish my day, and get paid for my 4 days. When I got my work permit very soon after, I quietly expressed my joy because some of my roommates had been waiting for their work permit for months.

I could go back to work at the restaurant, but August was coming to an end and I couldn't wait to find a school to enroll in. That's how I was able to quickly find a school, take the admissions tests and start classes on time. The only flaw was the hour and a half journey that separated me from the establishment. It took me several weeks to find an apartment in the same city and move in.

My understanding of the language was improving, and in the middle of the first year, I met my first boyfriend. We were both in first but in two different classes. He found me a little country, it is true that I had not yet grasped European dress codes and that I was lonely and spoke awkwardly. He was handsome and popular, and frequented me only outside of school.

He did not want to spoil his image of local celebrity, with his beautiful sports car and his reputation as executioner of hearts with the girls of the school. He was invited to all the parties, he was so cool that I fell in the panel.

I validated my first year and started the second. Since my boyfriend had little time for me and he barely spoke to me at school, I spent all my time waiting outside. I did not know how to do otherwise, I continued to wait.

I was assailed by the same eternal demons, the fear of speaking and of going to others, this unpleasant feeling that every time I tried to open my mouth, nothing was going right. The few times I have had to speak in class, my voice has been shaking systematically. It was really ridiculous, and I felt very guilty. Why was I not provided with the same ease with which everyone seemed to be endowed?

What was that thing that took my throat when I was trying to express something important? At first, I attributed this dysfunction to a trauma related to my mother's choice to forbid me to speak before Jesus returned, then I understood that it was only an excuse for me take responsibility for my own problems.

One day, I decided to end this handicap. After school, I rushed home and rushed to my computer, which had become my favorite pastime. In the search engine, I typed the following query: "How to get rid of shyness", I was told several videos, and readings that contained methods that I immediately put into practice. The solution lay in training, I had to force myself to raise my hand as many times as necessary, until it became a formality. The embarrassment was nothing, the article confirmed that ridicule had never killed anyone, the statistics were formal and unstoppable about it. Since the danger was non-existent, I started.

While I was in my roommate in the North Sea, my boyfriend intermittently contacted me saying that he was going to go on vacation, and that he would like to see me before leaving. I moved heaven and earth to get emergency leave for the next day, and when I broke, I ran to buy him a gift. It was a luxurious scent, I had never bought myself such a thing. That same evening, I hopped on a train to Liège to arrive two hours later at home and wait for it all night. When I finally got him on the phone, I recognized the voices of these girls who were still circling him, the very ones he loved to strut around in public.

They were all partying, he was drunk and forgot that we had to meet. When he finally arrived, I gave him his gift and kicked him out the door. I was tired of wasting my time with this shabby.

Eventually, I quickly found many other, much more rewarding activities and met new people, but spent considerable time glued to TV and computer screens.

I had always been fascinated by the channels that broadcast fashion shows and music videos, I dreamed of integrating this wonderful world of Show Business.

I was often told that I was way too thin. These African girls kept telling me that with such a size, I would never find a footballer boyfriend. They were crazy about these young athletes who had the coast. Personally, that meant absolutely nothing to me, but after hearing these criticisms of my body,

I began to eat a lot. I was ingesting tons of protein for athletes, it had become a real obsession, which produced no results. I finally came to my senses, convinced of the sterility of such worries.

FASHION

One day like any other, when I was happily surfing the Net, I saw the announcement of a fashion contest. I had little hope of becoming a model, not being tall enough. I still filled out the form with a photo attached. A few days later, I came across another ad that offered to go directly to the castings on the dates indicated. I asked a friend and former colleague for coffee to come with me. The day before, full of enthusiasm, I went to bed early after watching dozens of fashion TV shows. My friend refused to accompany me because of the snowy weather in December. I was scared, but I went to the casting and went all the way. I had to give a short interview, which was then posted online because I was selected for the first selection. Some people laughed at my accent, which discouraged me a little. I was affected as much by critics around me as by those of strangers. These unpleasantnesses never prevented me from continuing to want to overtake myself. Despite my self-restraint, I always went for it without turning around to meet my goals.

Shortly after, I received an email regarding my online registration for the first casting. My profile had been selected and I had to report to the next step. I couldn't believe it, it was an extraordinary event for me at that time. I had once again asked my friend to accompany me but this time it was the rain that held her back. The casting took place in a city center hotel. I entered my name at the entrance in exchange for a passage number and waited. There were few people in this small room. They made me fill in a paper my age, weight, height, shoe size, etc. Then I had a little discussion with the jury.

Then came the photo shoot. It was a very different cast from the previous one which had counted many more candidates, a larger staff and all in an imposing place.

The same evening, I received a strange sms from one of the staff members. I didn't really remember who it was. In his subsequent messages, he finally introduced himself. I took the opportunity to ask him if he could assess my chances of winning, he replied 95%. This estimate seemed abnormally high, but since I had no experience in the business, I contented myself with answering politely. He quickly offered me a video chat session, I accepted the first time and then understood that his intentions were not professional.

Two weeks later, I received a letter regarding the other cast informing me that I had been selected for the semi-final. In the envelope was attached a very nice photo of me taken on the day of the casting. I was literally mad with joy, I smiled continuously and uttered little cries of joy. Once the euphoria subsided, the big picture came back to my mind, I was selected for two competitions, I could do both but I preferred to choose the best and drop the other. Neither I nor my entourage could afford to resolve this difficult dilemma.

I put the letter away and went to clear my mind in the city, precisely in a shopping center. When I ran into a random shop assistant, I had the idea of talking to her about my situation and asking her for advice. After giving her the names of the two contests and explaining my doubt, she admitted that she was unable to help me. I took my leave to continue my walk, still smiling.

A promotional evening was organized for the discreet first competition. In the meantime, I had investigated the two competitions and the second, more substantial, seemed preferable to me.

In order to be sure, I went to the evening of the first one anyway. The general atmosphere betrayed its unprofessional character, the organizers were too close to the candidates.

After this evening, I and several candidates decided to leave the competition. Among these girls, there was a sympathetic Congolese, who since that day has remained a close friend.

I received the invitation for the first rehearsals of the semifinals in January 2011, they were held in a province difficult to access. The shooting stage went perfectly, and I made new friends who finally shared my passions. The photos were splendid but to keep them and build my Book, I had to acquire them. You also had to pay the participation fees for the semi-final or find a sponsor. I couldn't find a sponsor, and I also had a lot of trouble convincing my friends to come and support me on the day of the semi-final. Only a handful of them agreed to attend the event.

The quality rehearsals given by the organization were prolific. I had progressed enormously in record time. Day after day, I kept fueling myself with fashion shows that I followed tirelessly on TV, walking with high heels, a big dictionary on my head to stay straight. I had also taken a few Catwalk lessons through a fashion contact.

This semi-final was my first achievement, I was lucky to reach the final. This was followed by other rehearsals that lasted an entire weekend in the company of all the other candidates. All this had allowed me to meet good people, but I still couldn't find a sponsor.

So to make this great moment possible, I went back to plunge into a restaurant for an entire month.

Phenomenal final, the catwalk was sparkling and fashion stars were present. A few rare relatives came to support me, and for the others, I was seriously considering changing relationships. When I was parading, I didn't think of anything else, I was 100% concentrated in the present, just the opposite of the rest of my life.

It was the most glorious moment of my life, there was no more painful childhood, no more trauma attacks or nightmares. I was simply blessed. I never thought that such a feeling could exist, that such a feeling of gratitude for life could be possible.

I was used to living with the pain by my side, and I forgot about everything else possible. The lightness of a moment of ecstasy and its share of pleasant thoughts. It was as if I had spent reclusive years in a room with closed curtains and that one day someone had opened the curtains on a sunset that I discovered for the first time, as an indescribable happiness to handy.

What an immense joy I felt when I was announced as a second prize winner, I was in a dream. Since that day, I have continued to persevere in the areas that make me happy, all the gold in the world cannot replace this satisfaction.

However, this victory did not take off my career. I continued to take photos and fashion shows out of passion and sometimes for free, considering these activities as hobbies in addition to my studies. Many of my friends were unemployed and were not studying, I gradually stopped going to them. My ex-boyfriend from school was suddenly impressed by my recent activities and awards, and now wanted to strut around my arm like a trophy, too bad for him.

During my last year of study I was no longer working in the cafe, it was far too tiring and the goal of furnishing my apartment had been achieved. My Congolese friend I met in casting contacted me to find out if I was interested in a job as a hostess in chic parties. I liked the idea on paper, and she communicated my number to the recruiter, who offered me an appointment the same evening. He had to come and get me so that we could have a drink outside the city, in a quiet place. I was so naive and still am sometimes.

A hostess being judged on her appearance, I put on my 31 for the occasion, just to give a good first impression. I had given him an address close to my home, I did not want a stranger to know where I lived. He took me to some brewery to chat and explained to me what my role would be. My performance would take place in a champagne bar frequented by wealthy men who wanted young hostesses to keep them company. It was desirable to encourage them to consume in order to increase their commissions. He pointed out that after drinking, most asked to go up to a room with the hostess and added that it was strongly advised to accept, at the risk of obtaining only a minimal cachet. The conversation had taken an unpleasant turn, his authoritarian air had increased crescendo since the beginning of our exchange and I began to be a little scared. He gave me the names of several student girls I knew who worked for him and who offered everything they wanted: house, car, …

We were out of town and I bitterly regretted having accepted this meeting. He added that I could also recruit girls on my side and so I would get a percentage of their income. I understood at that time why my friend had contacted me. To prevent him from hurting me, I replied that I was interested. He offered to call someone who would test me the same evening.

I replied that I was too tired from my long day and that it was better to wait until the next day. He still insisted on showing me what one of these bars looked like, I was practically forced to accept. By some unknown providence, we arrived at a closed bar. It was a great relief when he brought me back to town. I offered to call him the next day in the middle of the day for a test appointment. What a beautiful escape, the next day I replied that I had changed my mind. Four years later, I came across a report about his arrest and that of several girls who fell into his clutches.

They hadn't had the chance to have a day to think about it, the night of the meeting, he would take them home to take the famous test. The rest was just harassment and intimidation to force them into prostitution.

Once I graduated from high school, I left Liège for Brussels on a whim. I was going to miss this city, I no longer shared the same vision as my friends and my best friend no longer spoke to me because she knew I was going to try to convince her to stop illegal activities she has started.

Brussels was much more dynamic and I quickly adapted to its pace.

I was able to take advantage of my vacation to explore it and think about what I was going to be able to do in higher education. I didn't want to get into long, time-consuming studies. I consulted an adviser to choose my option and the associated schools, my profile was oriented hotel, tourism and international trade.

I was given printed sheets containing the options I had chosen and their corresponding schools, all I had to do was register. I phoned my family the same evening to tell them of my choices, but the news did not produce the expected result. In their eyes, none of this was valid or serious, only the paramedical field was possible. I stood up to them out of habit but I realized that I had nothing to prove, I felt able to succeed in long and difficult studies. I enrolled in the faculty of economic sciences of the Free University of Brussels deemed arduous. I didn't worry because my previous results in economics had been pretty good. Fortunately, my accommodation was only a 6-minute walk from the university. From the start, I was quite interested in the courses that I attended assiduously and I adapted to the customs of folk student evenings. I saw myself, already at the end of my training, accessing a very good job in a bank.

My greatest passion, fashion, was always present. During my first year, I participated in a fashion competition in which one of the organizers, an extremely nice person, had become a friend. He had nothing in common with these numerous organizers mired in multitudes of scams. He was a humble man who administered his competition according to the rules of the art. I passed the semi-final and then the final and won a prize once again. Thanks to this competition, I was able to access an international competition which would take place in Turkey. It was my first trip abroad for fashion, this competition brought together candidates from all over the world. I was very impressed, Naomi Campbell had participated in these young years, the competition took place in early December, a month before the first exam session.

Two weeks before my departure, when I was putting my papers in order, I realized that my passport had only one week left. Cold shower, to get the visa on time I had to order a passport urgently. It cost four times the normal price, a huge amount for my student savings. Willing to do anything not to risk missing such an opportunity, I chose not to pay my rent that month.

This competition surpassed all that I had known before, I was intimidated, and my performance was not the most glorious. The stress had created a self-confidence deficit, which I had fought as best I could. Back in Belgium with my only pride of having participated in an international competition, reality came back to me; it was now necessary to save to pay the month's rent late.

I finished my first year with few successful exams, I kept hoping that everything would be better in the second session. After having camped for several weeks at the library, I still repeated. I could have changed options at that time, but I was taking this challenge to heart, I wanted to prove myself something, and immersed myself in the revisions, doubling the rate of my revisions.

To drive the point home, I completely abandoned the fashion world by cutting ties with people from this sector, I also took private lessons for certain subjects. I passed 80% of the exams in the first term, rested on my laurels, and missed the second. A week after the holidays started, I went back to the library, and after a few days, I had no motivation.

I have been studying for two years now without taking a vacation, with very few results. After analyzing my real chances of success and in response to this categorical assessment, I decided to stop my studies.

I had been interested in the positive psychology movement for a while and I read a lot of biographies about it. My outlook on the world had changed, and I was convinced that there was another way to succeed without taking the classic path. I sharpened my thoughts, keeping in mind that each negative situation held a pool of opportunities. Once again, I could no longer get along with my friends from Brussels with a narrow vision. I had opened my brain to a new way of thinking, I wanted to grow, grow, evolve, and we didn't have much in common. They were locked up in their little bickering while I envisioned the powers of our subconscious.

I was grateful to be alive, I wanted to discover inner peace. I had survived the genocide, then I had grown up, but I was still not at peace. I often cried at night thinking about the injustices that my family had suffered. As if I had kept my soul of a child and that at the slightest test, it sprang up taking control.

Thanks to my readings, I was able to understand and accept the events of the past as definitive and belonging to something beyond, finished.

Life gave me a second wind, and it had to be captured by breaking free from the weight of the past. In the same way, I managed to put my academic failure into perspective. It was absolutely nothing serious not to pass a course that would lead me to an office job in a bank, it was a dream that could easily be done. I could succeed in another branch, find my way elsewhere.

That summer, I felt like a wave of relief, I went on vacation to Spain to party. The tensions between my family and me were at climax, they wanted me to resume classes directly in another option, but I wanted to take a break. They didn't understand my dreams because they didn't understand who I was. They judged me irresponsible and it hurt me.

I was invited to the south of Spain to stay with the parents of a Spanish friend I met at the university. I had been able to save money on plane tickets by working in a bar a few months before. We spent our days at the beach taking pictures of ourselves, then we came back to get ready to go dancing in the evening, in a festive street in Marbella called Puerto Banus. All the boxes offered us tokens of drinks at the entrance, it was very easy for two young women to make no expense except for transport. Back in the morning, her mom served us a gazpacho to cushion our daily hangover.

The desire to return to the fashion world was quickly felt. That same summer, I represented myself in the casting of the competition made in 2012 during my first year of university. I wanted to relive the experience, I had a taste for travel, and I wanted to discover new cultures and new horizons. I went straight to the final stages, and we had the chance to work with a great photographer from the Dominique Models agency, Ercan Dedeoglu. His presence was a great pleasure, I followed all the indications with my finger and my eye. My enthusiasm was commensurate with the expected result, the photos were sensational, we were both very satisfied. He was a simple and humble man, far from the idea that I could have had of a photographer of such stature.

He was respectful while mastering the postures that could enhance my physiognomy, a practice very different from other amateur photographers with whom I had to work. He only selected two photos, and even today I consider them my best.

During this period, I had to find a permanent position in administration or in sales, I wanted to work, travel and what happened. After only two interviews, I got a human resources position with a government agency.

The contract was to start on January 1, 2015, so I had several weeks before me to prepare for it and participate in the competition.

At the time of the last rehearsals, we had to reserve seats for our guests, and pay the amount in advance. I've been wearing very short hair for two and a half years, I had the idea of selling all my hair maintenance equipment to pay for 3 places, that was the only solution. One of the organizers, a man of great generosity, who knew the extent of my commitment, let me take the places for the final later. Only two people took their tickets themselves.

The finale took place in a reception hall of a very luxurious hotel, it was a moment of great beauty, thanks, among other things, to the photos of Ercan which were disseminated during the ceremony. Surprisingly, I received two awards: a third place in my category, and the award for the model that worked best: "Best Catwalk". The painful repetitions in my living room with a dictionary on my head had not been useless, the more my experience accumulated, the more I improved.

Once again, what I sensed was confirmed, when you put your heart into it, no dream can resist, it comes true, sooner or later. The words I had read in Paulo Coelho's The Alchemist some time before resounded in my mind: "When you want something, the whole Universe conspires to allow you to realize your desire".

Thanks to the competition, I was selected to participate once again in the international competition. I also found a little job in a cafe to top up my account where tips most often exceeded my salary.

Unlike the first time, I was more relaxed about participating in this competition again. I was less stressed by the desire to win at all costs, I just wanted to live the experience and get the best out of it. I was more open to meeting other candidates with whom I spent pleasant moments. We were staying in a much more luxurious hotel in Istanbul than the previous time. One week before my departure, I had signed an employment contract for a position in the human resources of a government agency which would start three weeks after my return from Istanbul, everything seemed to be in perfect working order.

The overall atmosphere was more pleasant than the previous year, we visited historic places in Istanbul like Galatasaray, which according to legend is an island which was used as a hiding place for a princess to protect herself from a dragon. We sometimes spent whole days rehearsing, punctuated by a restaurant or a night out. A day before the final, members of the jury and a few photographers arrived at the hotel, and I found the delicious Ercan.

On the evening of the final, he sat at the large table of the jury made up of twenty personalities from around the world. To my surprise, I won once again the Best Catwalk award. It was then that I realized that I had made the right choice to come despite adversity, and that in the future I would seize every opportunity.

Back in Brussels, I was over the moon and impatient to start my new job. A few days later, Ercan contacted me to invite me to the casting of the dubbing of a big star for an advertisement. After a few exchanges, it turned out that I did not have the required measurements.

Despite everything, he informed me that he wanted to introduce myself to someone at Dominique Models. I had to read his message at least 10 times before I was sure it was real. I had already toured all the possible agencies, but none had wanted to represent me and I had given up.

I was content with freelance contracts. I replied with enthusiasm and three days later, I showed up for the meeting after a night of excitement. Once arrived, the person I was to meet was absent, I was very afraid that he had changed his mind in the meantime. I got a call from Ercan who offered me a new date for the next day. I met a woman in charge of a special department of the agency who offered to integrate me despite my 166 cm. I had the advantage of being exceptionally photogenic and with a face of character. It was this same face, through the intensity of its experience, that opened all the other doors to me. It seems that some people carry their souls on their faces, and I like to think that this is my case.

After the end of year celebrations, I was impatient to take my job. On the agency side, the shooting and publication of my profile on the website only took a few weeks, a new page opened. My human resources position was going well, I had a good salary, benefits, and flexible hours that allowed me to organize my fashion activities.

I always dreamed of traveling the world to drink of its cultures, thirsty for discoveries and new knowledge.

Each month, I set aside money dedicated to tourist trips. I started with the nearest countries, traveling alone for the sake of simplicity. I agreed to go with some friends in the summer to party, an activity that was generally more unifying and easily organized, but I never felt the systematic need to be part of groups. Already at school, I was not in any group and performed the sheepish mimicry of those I observed. I already knew what I wanted and preferred to decide how to organize my time, as it is limited and therefore precious, in the most efficient way possible.

Despite its undeniable advantages, the position of human resources quickly bored me. Learning the tasks had been tedious, it was a new field and my first serious professional experience. My role was divided between several departments, human resources, grants, internal communication, databases and regulations. I could be versatile but it was impossible to integrate into any of the services by always having to move to another, the concentration required not to mix the records of all these services was too important. I didn't have time to get bored, but I still spent my days counting hours, always waiting to be able to flee.

The seven-storey building had been built according to ecological criteria, one floor per department, and each floor was arranged in Open Space, all offices and rooms were open and equipped so that anyone could work there, no matter the hierarchy. This lack of privacy kept me from focusing on my work. Some days I settled on the sixth floor and others on the seventh, the only moments to take a break were tea or coffee breaks. At noon, I took the opportunity to run away. I took a bus and went to lunch with a friend who worked in an insurance company about ten minutes from my office.

The idea of spending all my days behind a computer increasingly displeased me. Fortunately, from time to time, the agency called me for castings or shootings. I didn't get contracts at the start, I was warned that it would take a little while. I remember this blessed day, a month after I started my new job, when the agency called me to offer me a first casting. What bliss! The casting was organized for an advertising campaign, I had bought new clothes and had rehearsed in front of my webcam a million times. When the day came, I took a taxi an hour in advance to make sure I got there on time.

Coming home from work this Friday, February 13, 2015, when I had to take the train the next day for a Valentine's Day weekend alone in Paris, I was informed that I had been chosen for the campaign. I imploded with joy.

This first job went wonderfully, I learned about the new rates accompanying my agency modeling services, the sum was dizzying. A few weeks later, the head of my department sent me a link to watch the advertising film that had just been released. I was blown away, happy, proud, and so many other emotions intertwined in me. I knew that I would never find so much satisfaction and pleasure in my other office work, and yet I had to keep it to ensure the stability of my existence.

I was thinking of all these other employees in my department and on the other floors of this huge boring building, and I was trying to imagine how many of them had forgotten, buried, or given up their dreams by agreeing to be financially protected, at the cost of boredom and permanent frustration. Maybe that's where all these conflicts came from, and the open plan offices shouldn't improve things. Certainly they had families to feed, and fights other than mine to wage. They had chosen routine rather than combat.

It was the longest year of my life. The seconds seemed to me hours and the hours, whole days.

My associates changed as my personal development progressed. Between my work and the frequent shootings, I still managed to organize a little trip. My first destination was Paris, which I visited several times afterwards, then came to Holland. For a person as eager for discovery as I am, who is not ashamed to assail the natives with questions, there is no better feeling of freedom. Being alone, I could choose exactly the activities I wanted, I liked taking the time to observe and think. I often asked my way to passersby who always seemed very happy to be able to help me.

In August 2015, in the south of France, I discovered the Côte d'Azur. Once there, a memory came to my mind. In 2013, I was contacted by a young woman who offered to participate in an international beauty contest in the French Riviera. Unfortunately, my professional activities at the time did not allow me to make myself available. In 2015, I had a few days of leave in reserve. So I got back in touch with this particularly affable young woman who quickly confirmed my participation as well as the high probability of winning a prize.

She was a former participant in the competition, and the first Rwandan to participate. She had assumed responsibility for hiring participants from her country.

I was about to fill out the papers when I learned that the country's official Miss had just contacted the organization. My chances of participating had just diminished, I did not hold the official title of Miss Rwanda, all I had to argue was my record. Miss Rwanda found no sponsor to finance her trip and participation. She gave up. I became the official representative of Rwanda for this competition. A stylist friend lent me two of these magnificent creations for the final performance; so far so good.

When my participation was confirmed, some of my photos ended up on the walls of the official competition's social networks. At the time, the Rwandan press was developing at high speed, the scoop race was intense. Many articles about me quickly emerged, I expected to be supported, but it was far from being the case. Each official candidate had to provide the organization with several photos, including one in a swimsuit, which I did. In Rwanda, posing in a swimsuit is seen as an offense against good character and decency.

Before me, only those who were not from Rwanda wore a swimsuit during the competition. The Rwandan women, afraid of having the Rwandan press on their backs, preferred to wear something to cover their bodies.

I was determined to fight this habit. When you make the choice to participate in a competition, you must be ready to submit to the rules that govern it, otherwise participating would no longer make sense. Several Rwandan newspapers repeated the same inappropriate titles about me, and my photos in bikinis became the subject of the month. I did not understand their relentlessness on an element as minimal as a swimsuit, when it would have been better to use this media frenzy to support the candidate of their country. The articles were certainly shocking, but what saddened me the most were cruel and insulting comments from anonymous people. After a day or two, I made up my mind and it didn't matter to me anymore, I was certainly not going to change my way of seeing things in response to their vehemence. Their opinion no longer mattered to me, I wanted to take full advantage of this competition and give the best.

The second part of the competition took place in Poland until the final on December 5, 2015. I had been wearing very short hair for over 4 years, and I had taken care to go to the hairdresser before the competition. The competition lasted two weeks, and my three suitcases included everything to enhance my brilliance. The competition was not what really motivated me, it was the simple fact of traveling, of going somewhere, which delighted me. Not going to work all this time was also something to be appreciated. I finally understood how my employed friends felt when I was a student, telling myself that student life was a blessing. Their theory was not entirely valid, but I understood that a satisfying job would not fill a life, or solve all other problems. What I had deeply integrated, on the other hand, was that it was essential for the body and the mind to act in an area that we love with passion.

The plane landed at dusk, a driver was waiting for me with the Swiss candidate that I got to know during our trip to the hotel.

Most of the other candidates had arrived three days ago, but we were not the last. The winter in Poland seemed much rougher than in Belgium.

Well before discovering our rooms, we were informed of the planning for the following days. I was surprised to learn that I was among the small number of candidates selected for their photogenics to participate in the photo session of the great Warsaw Exhibition which would take place in a sumptuous museum. We then discovered our rooms and unlike others, I was happily alone in mine.

The next morning's alarm sounded early, I was part of the group that left first. We stayed all day at the museum, the makeup lasted for hours and then we went to dressing and hairdressing. Coming home in the evening, we discovered the program for the next day, then we had dinner and went to bed. The next day everything accelerated, the rehearsals, the parades, and after a few busy days we left Warsaw for Krakow, where we stayed for a while. Then we joined the south-east of Poland, Krynica-Zdroj, where I shared a huge suite with four very nice candidates. Only a few days separated us from the final stages.

The elimination stages gave birth to the first moments of suspense and tension and I got my place in the top ten of the Top Models profiles.

The Rwandan Press followed the competition very closely, their love for me fluctuated with the sandstone of potentially exploitable scandals or my relative success. Meanwhile, the content of our days alternated between long rehearsals and tourist activities. The most memorable was that of the city of Kraków and its charming little authentic Jewish districts, unfortunately emptied by the Shoah, then recently rebuilt. It had particularly touched me with the sure empathy I could feel. Krakow reasoned in me like a city with a particular atmosphere, loaded with an omnipresent weight.

The cold imposed its icy grip, but nothing could prevent me from enjoying all these events. During this time, my Brussels friends had informed me of the chaos caused by the recent terrorist acts in Belgium, schools and shops had closed their doors as a precaution.

Being away from the violence of the world was reassuring. The day of the final was near, the pressure was palpable. The online media had already launched their predictions and I always found myself in the top ten or twenty. The decisive day arrived, excitement and fatigue fought for the rest of my strength.

The scenography of this finale was sumptuous and sensational.

During the few hours that preceded this great moment, in addition to the countless rehearsals, we had to go get our national costumes and come back to have our makeup and hair done. Some candidates had welcomed family members who came to support them. For me there was nobody. I had seen many others, it did not matter to me at all now, I had learned a long time ago to draw strength from me. The final was broadcast live on a national channel and on the web. Three big stages led to the crowning, three eliminatory presentations which I won one after the other until the final victory. I became Miss of all African countries, Miss Supra-National. It was the first time that Rwanda had won this competition, and it remained the greatest prize that a miss could win for my country.

It was a personal victory at the same time as that of an entire country, my pride and my happiness were indisputable. The end of the ceremony was a procession of compliments, smiles, autographs, hugs, congratulations and photos.

I was particularly moved to meet all these children who told me they wanted to become a miss and win prizes, what moments of happiness! Then we all went to the big party in a hotel reception hall and I was able to greet each person individually.

I slept very little that night because my return flight took off at dawn. I had received an incredible amount of congratulatory messages, many of them from strangers.

The return was trying, and at the same time, I felt that I would miss these precious moments. These three weeks had passed like a bullet. When I got home, I added this new crown to my price collection. I was proud to be victorious, and most of all, I was proud to have kept my motivation despite the constant pressure from the press. I had remained adamant and strong, certain of my choices and my convictions.

Several days after the competition, I continued to receive many congratulatory messages.

When I think of my journey, I can't help but analyze the different types of personalities that I have come across on my way. I have noticed that some people have a propensity to project their anxieties and worries onto those who want to try big things.

They want to discourage them to reassure themselves. But once these projects are completed, these same people will be the first to spread endless praise. Knowing this, I now preferred to keep my personal projects secret until a certain point in their evolution, in order to avoid arousing the disapproval of some demotivating people by nature.

My life resumed its course and I returned to my work, there were only a few weeks left before my contract ended. This prospect rejoiced, I was going to be able to rest and then travel again. Some time later, I passed my driver's license, and found another part-time job in a clothing store. The ready-to-wear store was located on a street full of luxury brands, it was perfect for me, I enjoyed meeting and advising customers. I didn't care that my kindness could be seen as a weakness. Ignoring dictates has been my strength for some time.

In October 2016, I went to the USA as a representative of Rwanda on an international podium. It was my first time in this country, starting with a month in New York and its surroundings. What immeasurable panoramas and what unlimited wonders!

On the way to Las Vegas, we crossed the rocky mountains and the grand canyon of Arizona, I was obviously amazed from start to finish.

The Red Rock Canyon was of such splendor that I was dazzled for a long time. There, I met and spoke to a large number of people who heard and heard for the first time in East Africa, there is a small country called Rwanda.

There is still a long way to go, and my lucky star continues to shine more. Since my beginnings, I collaborated with several prestigious brands, made the cover of fashion magazines, and day by day, this passion always feeds my desire to surpass myself. Today, I live in London and my contracts are multiplied. I collaborate with agencies in France, the United Kingdom, Belgium, Switzerland, Portugal, Bulgaria,... I posed for Cartier, Dolce & gabanna,

Gucci, Yves-saint-laurent, Moschino, Dior, ... I have made several appearances in magazines such as Grazia, Amica, Diva, Woman today, Pollen mag, ... In 2019, I made several magazine covers and one of my favorite sessions was that with the Belgian Photographer Jonas Leriche. It was an artistic session for a Louis Vuiton aesthetic concept. The large format photos were framed and exhibited in major art galleries in New York, London, Mykonos, ... one of them was bought by the famous singer The Weeknd and on the cover of a large luxury magazine published in Milan for its January 2019 edition available at all airports.

My greatest pride was to receive messages from friends posing next to my commercials. Recently, I had the chance to participate in parades of new designer collections such as the talented Sherri Hill.

I was also part of several advertising campaigns for cosmetic, jewelry and clothing brands such as Avon London, Zalando, G-star raw among others and the road continues... In the near future, I have the ambitious project of creating my own line of clothing and handbags for women.

Many people wonder about my eternal good humor: "How do you manage to display a perpetual smile and love life with everything you have gone through? I answer that I have even more reasons to smile. When you escape death you learn the value of each moment, and over time, the past no longer seems so terrible. I am proud to have walked this unique path which is mine. Take the story of a friend who was shot in the back during the massacres. Healed from her injury, she now has a huge scar visible only when she undresses. I never heard her talk about it or complain about it. Only the scar was invisible and invisible to her. Only the others saw her.

My gaze travels through the solid blue of the sky, the future looks bright.

Interahamwe: means in Kinyarwanda "People who get along very well" or "People of the same generation" according to the dictionary. These militias were responsible for most of the massacres during the genocide in 1994.

Kunywana: Ritual performed by two Rwandans who wanted to unite by promising themselves a loyal friendship. It was customary to make a small cut on the stomach, then each drank the other's blood. Whoever betrays the pact is killed with ferocity.

Inkotanyi: Fierce warrior.

Tutsi: Population living in the African Great Lakes region. Minority group in Rwanda and Burundi. Historically often called: Watutsi, Watusi, Wahuma or Wahima.

Hutu: Bantu population of central Africa, which constituted the majority group in Rwanda and Burundi, 85% of the total population.

Bibliography

Alexis. K. Inganji karinga, deuxième édition, Kabgayi
NSANZABERA. JD. , Imizi y'u Rwanda, Kigali 2013
WIKIPEDIA. , Histoire du Rwanda
AMBASSADE DU RWANDA. , géographie du Rwanda,
site internet COELHO. P. , L'Archimiste,

128